KNOLE
AND THE SACKVILLES

KNOLE
AND THE SACKVILLES

By V. SACKVILLE-WEST

ERNEST BENN LIMITED
LONDON & TONBRIDGE

Published by Ernest Benn Limited
25 New Street Square, London EC4A 3JA
& Sovereign Way, Tonbridge, Kent TN9 1RW

First published 1922
Second Edition 1923
Second Impression 1926
Third Impression 1930
Fourth Impression 1931
Fifth Impression 1934
Third Edition 1947
Second Impression 1948
Third Impression 1949
Fourth Edition 1958
Second Impression 1969
Third Impression 1973
Fourth Impression 1976

Printed in Great Britain

ISBN 0 510–27901–5

FOREWORD

THIS book was first published in 1922. Since it was written some new information has been provided in two massive volumes entitled *History of the Sackville Family, together with a description of Knole and early owners of Knole*, by Charles J. Phillips, published by Cassell & Co., Ltd., at eight guineas. Mr. Phillips, over a period of nearly ten years, undertook much original research at his own expense, employing readers to go through the manuscripts at Lambeth Palace, the Record Office, the British Museum, and the Diocesan Library at Canterbury; personally investigating some of the contents of the Muniment Room at Knole; and consulting such sources as the Pipe Rolls, the Charter Rolls, the Patent Rolls, the Close Rolls, and the reports of the Historical Manuscripts Commission. Had I possessed the common sense and patience to wait for the publication of Mr. Phillips's immense work, my own book would have been far more amply informed. But Mr. Phillips, so thorough and conscientious, was at the same time extremely dilatory and endearingly vague. He would lend me large lumps of his manuscript somewhat illegibly hand-written on foolscap paper, and never seemed to want them back. There were moments when I wondered whether his book would ever come out at all.

For these reasons I decided to go ahead with the publication of my own book in 1922.

The resetting of the type in this new edition in 1958 gives me the opportunity of incorporating a few alterations, corrections, and additions, and also some material which has come to my notice over the course of years.

V. S.-W.

ACKNOWLEDGEMENTS

My thanks are due to *Country Life* for the photographs of the Green Court, the Stone Court, the Venetian Ambassador's Bedroom, the Brown Gallery, the Leicester Gallery, and the Spangle Bedroom; to Derek Adkins for the Stone Court and the Great Hall; to Messrs. Geo. P. King, Ltd., of Sevenoaks, for the North-east view, the garden side, the Cartoon Gallery, the Great Staircase, Lady Betty Germain's Bedroom, and the portraits of Lady Betty Germain, the 4th Earl of Dorset, his two sons, the 6th Earl of Dorset, Lady Anne Clifford, the 3rd Duke of Dorset, and the Three Children; to the National Portrait Gallery for the *Somerset House Conference* 1604; to Aero Pictorial Ltd., for two air-photographs of Knole; and to Margaret Countess of Suffolk and Berkshire for permission to reproduce the portrait of Richard, 3rd Earl of Dorset, by Daniel Mytens.

V. S.-W.

Sissinghurst Castle, Kent
April 1958

CONTENTS

CHRONOLOGICAL TABLE

Thomas Sackville, LORD BUCKHURST, 1st EARL of DORSET, K.G., 1536–1608

1603 Death of Queen Elizabeth. Succeeded by JAMES I
1603 Lord Treasurer for life
1604 Created Earl of Dorset
1608 Death at the Council Table

Robert Sackville, 2nd EARL of DORSET, 1561–1609

1579 Married MARGARET HOWARD, daughter of 4th Duke of
       NORFOLK
1585⎫
1608⎭ Member of Parliament
1592 Married ANNE SPENCER
1608 Succeeded his father, THOMAS
1609 Death

Richard Sackville, 3rd EARL of DORSET, 1589–1624

1609 Married ANNE CLIFFORD, daughter of GEORGE, 3rd EARL
       OF CUMBERLAND
1609 Succeeded his father, ROBERT
1624 Death

Edward Sackville, 4th EARL of DORSET, K.G., 1589 (*or* '90)–1652

1605 At Christ Church, Oxford
1612 Married MARY, daughter of SIR GEORGE CURZON
1614 His duel with LORD BRUCE
1614 Member of Parliament
1621 Ambassador to LOUIS XIII
1623⎫
1624⎭ Travels in Italy
1623 Again Ambassador to LOUIS XIII
1624 Succeeded his brother, RICHARD
1624 Lord-Lieutenant of Sussex and Middlesex
1625 Death of James I. Succeeded by CHARLES I
1628 Lord Chamberlain
1630 Lady Dorset appointed Governess to the King's children
1631⎫
1634⎭ Commissioner for Planting Virginia
1638 Granted the East Coast of America
1642 Outbreak of civil war. Lord Dorset joins the KING at
       York
1644 Lord Privy Seal
1649 Execution of CHARLES I
1652 Death

Richard Sackville, 5th EARL of DORSET, 1622–1677

1637   Married FRANCES CRANFIELD, daughter of LIONEL, EARL OF MIDDLESEX
1652   Succeeded his father, EDWARD
1670   Lord-Lieutenant of Sussex
1677   Death

Charles Sackville, 6th EARL of DORSET and EARL of MIDDLESEX, K.G., 1637 (*or* '36)–1706

1660   Member of Parliament
1660   Restoration of CHARLES II
1668   Ambassador to France
1674   Death of his mother; he succeeds to the Cranfield estates
1675   Created EARL OF MIDDLESEX
1677   Succeeded his father, RICHARD, as EARL OF DORSET
1678   Married MARY, COUNTESS OF FALMOUTH
1685   Married MARY COMPTON, daughter of JAMES, EARL OF NORTHAMPTON
1685   Death of Charles II. Succeeded by JAMES II
1688   Accession of MARY and WILLIAM OF ORANGE
1689)
1697)   Lord Chamberlain
1701   His poems published with SEDLEY'S
1702   Death of William III. Succeeded by QUEEN ANNE
1704   Married ANNE ROCHE
1706   Death

Lionel Sackville, 7th EARL and 1st DUKE of DORSET, K.G., 1688–1765

1706   Succeeded his father, CHARLES, as EARL OF DORSET and MIDDLESEX
1709   Married ELIZABETH COLYEAR
1708   Lord Warden of the Cinque Ports, intermittently till 1728
1714   Death of Queen Anne. Succeeded by GEORGE I
1720   Created Duke of Dorset
1725   Lord Steward
1727   Death of George I. Succeeded by GEORGE II
1730   Lord-Lieutenant of Ireland till 1737
1746   Lord-Lieutenant of Kent
1750   Lord-Lieutenant of Ireland till 1755
1760   Death of George II. Succeeded by GEORGE III
1765   Death

Charles Sackville, 2nd DUKE of DORSET, 1711–1769

Before 1734. On the Grand Tour
1734 Member of Parliament intermittently till 1754. Lord o
the Treasury and Master of the Horse
1744 Married GRACE BOYLE
1765 Succeeded his father, LIONEL
1769 Death

John Frederick Sackville, 3rd DUKE of DORSET, K.G.,
1745–1799

1769 Succeeded his uncle, CHARLES
1783}
1789} Ambassador to LOUIS XVI
1769}
1797} Lord-Lieutenant of Kent
1789}
1799} Lord Steward
1790 Married ARABELLA DIANA, daughter of SIR JOHN COPE
1799 Death

George John Frederick Sackville, 4th DUKE of DORSET,
1794–1815

1799 Succeeded his father, JOHN FREDERICK
1815 Death

LIST OF ILLUSTRATIONS

(All illustrations are placed between pages 128 and 129)

TABLE OF DESCENT

HERBRAND DE SACKVILLE, *temp.* **William the Conqueror**

SIR RICHARD SACKVILLE, *temp.* **Henry VIII**

THOMAS SACKVILLE *m. Cicely, dau. of Sir John Baker of Sissinghurst*
b. 1536   *d.* 1608
LORD BUCKHURST   *and*
1st EARL *of* DORSET, K.G.
ROBERT SACKVILLE *m. Lady Margaret Howard*
b. 1561   *d.* 1609
2nd EARL *of* DORSET

RICHARD SACKVILLE *m. Lady Anne Clifford*
b. 1589   *d.* 1624
3rd EARL *of* DORSET, K.G.

EDWARD SACKVILLE *m. Mary Curzon*
b. 1589 *or* '90   *d.* 1652
4th EARL *of* DORSET, K.G.

RICHARD SACKVILLE *m. Lady Frances Cranfield*
b. 1622   *d.* 1677
5th EARL *of* DORSET
CHARLES SACKVILLE *m.* (1) *Mary Bagot,* (2) *Lady Mary Compton,* (3) *Anne Roche*
b. 1637 *or* '36   *d.* 1706
6th EARL *of* DORSET, K.G.

LIONEL SACKVILLE *m. Elizabeth Colyear*
b. 1686   d. 1765
7th EARL *and*
1st DUKE *of* DORSET,
K.G.

CHARLES SACKVILLE
b. 1711   d. 1769
2nd DUKE *of* DORSET

LORD JOHN SACKVILLE
d. 1765

JOHN FREDERICK SACKVILLE
m. Arabella Diana Cope
b. 1745   d. 1799
3rd DUKE *of* DORSET, K.G.

LORD GEORGE SACKVILLE
b. 1716   d. 1785
cr. VISCOUNT SACKVILLE

CHARLES SACKVILLE
b. 1767   d. 1843
5th DUKE *of* DORSET, K.G.

LADY ELIZABETH SACKVILLE
m. John West, 5th Earl de la Warr   d. 1870
b. 1796

GEORGE JOHN FREDERICK SACKVILLE
b. 1794   d. 1815   4th DUKE *of* DORSET

WILLIAM EDWARD
b. 1837   d. 1905

LADY MARY SACKVILLE
m. (1) *the 6th Earl of Plymouth*
(2) *William Pitt, Earl Amherst*

CHARLES
EARL DE LA WARR
d. 1873

MORTIMER
1st LORD SACKVILLE
b. 1820   d. 1888

LIONEL
2nd LORD SACKVILLE
b. 1827   d. 1908

LIONEL
3rd LORD SACKVILLE
b. 1867   d. 1930

CHARLES
4th LORD SACKVILLE
b. 1870   d. 1962

V. SACKVILLE-WEST
b. 1892   d. 1962

EDWARD SACKVILLE-WEST
b. 1901   d. 1965

The dome of Knole, by fame enrolled,
  The Church of Canterbury,
The hops, the beer, the cherries there,
  Would fill a noble story.

Let Se'noaks vaunt the hospitable seat
  Of Knoll (sic) *most ancient; awfully my Muse*
These social scenes of grandeur and delight,
  Of love and veneration let me tread.
How oft beneath yon oak has am'rous Prior
  Awakened Echo with sweet Chloe's name,
While noble Sackville heard, hearing approv'd,
  Approving greatly recompens'd.

CHRISTOPHER SMART

CHAPTER I

THE HOUSE

§ i

THERE are two sides from which you may first profitably look at the house. One is from the park, the north side. From here the pile shows best the vastness of its size; it looks like a mediæval village. It is heaped with no attempt at symmetry; it is sombre and frowning; the grey towers rise; the battlements cut out their square regularity against the sky; the buttresses of the old twelfth-century tithe-barn give a rough impression of fortifications. There is a line of trees in one of the inner courtyards, and their green heads show above the roofs of the old breweries; but although they are actually trees of a considerable size they are dwarfed and unnoticeable against the mass of the buildings blocked behind them. The whole pile soars to a peak which is the clock-tower with its pointed roof: it might be the spire of the church on the summit of the hill crowning the mediæval village. At sunset I have seen the silhouette of the great building stand dead black on a red sky; on moonlight nights it stands black and silent, with glinting windows, like an enchanted castle. On misty autumn nights I have seen it emerging partially from the trails of vapour, and heard the lonely roar of the red deer roaming under the walls.

§ ii

The other side is the garden side—the gay, princely side, with flowers in the foreground; the grey walls rising straight up from the green turf; the mullioned windows, and the Tudor gables with the heraldic leopards sitting stiffly at each corner. The park side is the side for winter; the garden side the side for summer. It has an indescribable gaiety and courtliness. The grey of the Kentish rag is almost pearly in the sun, the occasional coral festoon of a climbing rose dashed against it;

the long brown-red roofs are broken by the chimney-stacks with their slim, peaceful threads of blue smoke mounting steadily upwards. One looks down upon the house from a certain corner in the garden. Here is a bench among a group of yews—dark, red-berried yews; and the house lies below one in the hollow, lovely in its colour and its serenity. It has all the quality of peace and permanence; of mellow age; of stateliness and tradition. It is gentle and venerable. Yet it is, as I have said, gay. It has the deep inward gaiety of some very old woman who has always been beautiful, who has had many lovers and seen many generations come and go, smiled wisely over their sorrows and their joys, and learnt an imperishable secret of tolerance and humour. It is, above all, an English house. It has the tone of England; it melts into the green of the garden turf, into the tawnier green of the park beyond, into the blue of the pale English sky; it settles down into its hollow amongst the cushioned tops of the trees; the brown-red of those roofs is the brown-red of the roofs of humble farms and pointed oast-houses, such as stain over a wide landscape of England the quilt-like pattern of the fields. I make bold to say that it stoops to nothing either pretentious or meretricious. There is here no flourish of architecture, no ornament but the leopards, rigid and vigilant. The stranger may even think, upon arrival, that the front of the house is disappointing. It is, indeed, extremely modest. There is a gate-house flanked by two square grey towers, placed between two wings which provide only a monotony of windows and gables. It is true that two or three fine sycamores, symmetrical and circular as open umbrellas, redeem the severity of the front, and that a herd of fallow deer, browsing in the dappled shade of the trees, maintains the tradition of an English park. But, for the rest, the front of the house is so severe as to be positively uninteresting; it is quiet and monkish; "a beautiful decent simplicity," said Horace Walpole, "which charms one." There is here to be found none of the splendour of Elizabethan building. A different impression, however, is in store when once the wicket-gate has been opened. You are in a courtyard of a size the frontage had never led you to expect, and the vista through a second gateway shows you the columns of a second court; your eye is caught by an oriel window opposite, and by other windows with heraldic bearings in their panes, promise of rooms and galleries; by gables and the heraldic leopards; by the clock tower which gives an oddly Chinese effect immediately above the Tudor oriel. Up till a few years ago Virginia creeper blazed scarlet in autumn on the walls of the Green Court, but it has now been torn away, and what may be lost in colour is compensated by the gain in seeing the grey stone and the slight moulding which runs, following the shape of the towers, across the house.

On the whole, the quadrangle is reminiscent of Oxford, though more palatial and less studious. The house is built round a system of these courtyards: first this one, the Green Court, which is the largest and most magnificent; then the second one, or Stone Court, which is not turfed, like the Green Court, but wholly paved, and which has along one side of it a Jacobean colonnade; the third court is the Water Court, and has none of the display of the first two: it is smaller, and quite demure, indeed rather like some old house in Nuremberg, with the latticed window of one of the galleries running the whole length of it, and the friendly unconcern of an immense bay-tree growing against one of its walls. There are four other courts, making seven in all. This number is supposed to correspond to the days in the week; and in pursuance of this conceit there are in the house fifty-two staircases, corresponding to the weeks in the year, and three hundred and sixty-five rooms, corresponding to the days. I cannot truthfully pretend that I have ever verified these counts, and it may be that their accuracy is accepted solely on the strength of the legend; but, if this is so, then it has been a very persistent legend, and I prefer to sympathize with the amusement of the ultimate architect on making the discovery that by a judicious juggling with his additions he could bring courts, stairs, and rooms up to that satisfactory total.

A stone lobby under the oriel window divides the Green Court from the Stone Court. In summer the great oak doors of this second gate-house are left open, and it has sometimes happened that I have found a stag in the banqueting hall, puzzled but still dignified, strayed in from the park since no barrier checked him.

It becomes impossible, after passing through the formality of the two first quadrangles, to follow the ramblings of the house geographically. They are so involved that, after a life-time of familiarity, I still catch myself pausing to think out the shortest route from one room to another. Four acres of building is no mean matter.

§ iii

Into the early mediæval history of the house I do not think that I need enter. It is suggested that a Roman building once occupied the site, and that some foundations which were recently unearthed beneath the larder—evidently one of the oldest portions—once formed part of that construction. The question of dating the existing buildings, however, is quite sufficiently complicated without going back to a possible Roman villa which no longer exists. Nor do I think that the early owners—even if we knew precisely who they were and what parts of the house we owe to them severally, would be of much interest. The mediæval records are very scanty. There is no documentary evidence to prove Knole ever belonged to the Earls of Pembroke. The first known reference to Knole is found in the Lambeth Palace papers for 1281, where it is found belonging to two un-explained persons calling themselves William and Roger de Knole. It is safe to say, generally speak-ing, that the north side is the oldest side; it is the most sombre, the most massive, and the most irregular; there are buttresses, battlements, and towers, but no gables and no embellishments —nothing but solid masonry. Up in the north-east corner is the old kitchen, and the old entrances through dark archways at the top of stairways. The passages here, of thick stone, twist oddly and their ceilings are groined by semi-arches which have become lost and embedded in the alterations to the stone-work. It is a dark, massive, little-visited corner, this nucleus of Knole.

The house, or such portions of it as existed in the fifteenth century, was bought from William Fiennes, Lord Saye and Sele, by Bourchier, Archbishop of Canterbury, on June 30, 1456, and it is clear from the numerous bills among the archives at Lambeth Palace that both he and his more notable successor, Cardinal Morton, carried out extensive additions, alterations, and repairs. It is, however, a very difficult task to determine what parts of the building definitely belong to this period, for, what with the additions of the Archbishops and the alterations of the later Sackvilles, all is confusion. It would appear, for instance, that upon a foundation of Tudor masonry the Sackvilles constructed the Elizabethan gables which are now so characteristic a feature of the house; but it is less easy to say exactly how much the first Tudor Archbishop found there on his arrival of earlier workmanship. A further confusing factor is the great fire which took place in 1623, and is reported to have destroyed a large part of the building—but exactly where, and how much, we cannot say. Nor are the accounts at Lambeth very illuminating:

In divers costs and expenses made this year [1467] for repairing the manor of Knole, carriage for the two cart loads of lathes from Panters to the manor, 14d. For carriage of thirty loads of stone for the new tower, 7d. load = 16/9. Carriage of six loads of timber at 7d. = 3/6. Carriage of one other of lead from London to Knole, 3/4.

The next year, 1468:

Repairs at Knole. One labourer for 6 days work in the great chamber and the new *seler*, 2/-. Making of 700 lathes to the new tower, 14d. One labourer 4½ days in the old kitchen, 4d. Item, for 1 j M[1] of walle prygge (*sic*) to the stable and other places, 13d. One cowl to the masonry, 12d.

The "great chamber" referred to here was in all probability the present Great Hall, which we know to have been built by Bourchier about 1460, although it was altered by Thomas Sackville, who put in the present ceiling, panelling, and oak screen. Thomas also built the Great Staircase in 1604–8, leading to the Ballroom, which is of the time of Bourchier. I expect this is the "seler" referred to, meaning solar and not cellar, as might be thought; or did it mean the present colonnade, which is also of Bourchier's building, in 1468? The position of the "new tower" is nowhere specified, but I wonder whether it is not the tower beside the chapel, where there is a stone fireplace bearing Bourchier's cognisance—the double knot—and the same device in a small pane of stained glass in the window. This tower, moreover, goes commonly by the name of Bourchier's Tower.

There are a few more items mentioned in the Lambeth papers, 1468-9: "Repairs at Knole. Repairs at one house set aside for the slaughter of sheep and other [animals?] for the use of the Lord's great house at Sevenoaks, 113s. 2d." This, I think, is certainly the old slaughter-house which forms one side of the Queen's Court. It is obviously a very old building. But there is one point in this account which is of interest, namely, that Knole should at this date have been referred to as the "great house." This would seem to prove that the greater mass of the building was already in existence, since by the latter half of the fifteenth century there were already many houses and palaces in England whose bulk would argue that the current standard of greatness might be high and the adjective not too readily applied. The Primate owned, moreover, up to the time of the Reformation no less than twelve palaces and houses of residence in the diocese of Canterbury alone, namely, Bekesburn, Ford, Maidstone, Charing, Saltwood, Aldington, Wingham, Wrotham, Tenterden, Knole, Otford, and Canterbury. It seems, therefore, unlikely that Knole should be singled out as a "great house" unless there were good justification for the expression.

Bourchier also built the Brown Gallery about 1460, and at or about the same date he put up the machicolations over the gate-house between the Green Court and the Stone Court. Towards the end of the same century, Morton, his successor, "threw out an oriel window which rendered the machicolations useless, and showed that all idea of such fortifications was at an end." It is not known precisely how much Morton built at Knole. It seems curious that if Morton did much building, he should not have used his usual rebus, a tun, or cask, with an M on it. It is even uncertain whether he or Bourchier built the Chapel. The Lambeth records cease with some small repairs in 1487–88, so we have nothing to go upon —all the more pity, for Morton was a great prelate, forgotten now in the greater fame of the Tudor dynasty, "his name buried," says his chronicler, "under his own creation." This cardinal, having succeeded Bourchier in 1486, held the Primacy for fourteen years, and died at Knole in 1500. I pass over his successors, Dean and Wareham, for I do not know how much they did at Knole. Cranmer, the next Archbishop, enjoyed the house for seven years only, when he was compelled—quite amicably, but nevertheless compelled—to present it to Henry VIII, whose fancy it had taken. Cranmer's secretary, Ralph Norice, gives an account of the transaction as he heard it:

My Lord, minded to have retained Knole unto himself, said that it was too small a house for his Majesty. Marry, said the King, I had rather have it than this house, meaning Otford; for it standeth on a better soil. This house standeth low, and is rheumatick, like unto Croydon, where I could never be without sickness. And as for Knole, it standeth on a sound, perfect, and wholesome ground; and if I should make abode here, as I do surely mind to do now and then, I will live at Knole and most of my house shall live at Otford. And so by this means both those houses were delivered into the King's hands.

Here the accounts begin again,[1] although they give very little indication: £872 by Royal Warrant in 1543, £770 in 1548, £80 in 1546—three sums which would now be equivalent, roughly, to £30,000.

After Henry VIII Knole continued as Crown property, passing now and then temporarily into the hands of various favourites, until in 1586 it was given by Queen Elizabeth to her cousin, Thomas Sackville, and has remained in the possession of his family ever since. (See, however, Appendix 2, on p. 215).

[1] State papers of Henry VIII.

§ iv

The main block, therefore, meanders from Henry VII through Henry VIII to Elizabeth and James I: that is to say, roughly, from the end of the fifteenth century to the beginning of the seventeenth. There may be earlier out-buildings and later excrescences, but it is safe to say that the greater portion was built in the reigns of the Tudors. It is all of the same Kentish rag, with the exception of a row of gables which have been plastered over, and which were probably once of the beam-and-plaster fashion so prevalent at that date in Kent. With this exception the walls are of the grey stone, in many places ten and twelve feet thick, cool in summer, and, for some reason, not particularly warm in winter. The rooms are, for the most part, rather small and rather low; they break out, of course, now into galleries, now into a ball-room, now into a banqueting-hall, but the majority of them are small, friendly rooms—not intimidating; some people might even think them poky, relative to the size of the house. I do not think that they are poky. They are eminently rooms intended to be lived in, and not merely admired, though no doubt a practical consideration was present in the problem of heating to determine their size. Yet from an old diary preserved at Knole, and from which in its place I shall have the opportunity to give extracts, it is clear that in the early seventeenth century the life of the house was carried on largely in one or the other of the long galleries. None of the galleries has more than one fireplace. It must have been very cold. The old braziers that could be carried about the room as occasion required still stand in the rooms where they were used, and so do the copper warming-pans, shining and perforated, which were thrust into the beds to warm them before the arrival of the occupant. The principal beds must have been magnificently stuffy. They are four-posters, so tall as to reach from floor to ceiling, with stiff brocaded curtains that could completely enclose the sleeper. But on winter days I cannot believe that the group ever moved very far away from the fireplace or the

brazier; and indeed, judging from the same diary, they seemed
always to be "keeping their chamber" on account of coughs,
colds, rheumatism, or ague when they were not keeping it
because they were "sullen" with one another, or "brought to
bed" of a son or a daughter.

§ v

The galleries are perhaps the most characteristic rooms in
such a house.

Long and narrow, with dark shining floors, armorial glass
in the windows, rich plasterwork ceilings, and portraits on
the walls, they are splendidly sombre and sumptuous. The
colour of the Cartoon Gallery, when I have come into it in
the evening, with the sunset flaming through the west window, has often taken my breath away. I have stood, stock still
and astonished, in the doorway. The gallery is ninety feet in
length, the floor formed of black oak planks irregularly laid,
the charm of which is that they are not planks at all, but solid
tree-trunks, split in half, with the rounded half downwards;
so is the tradition, and I like to believe it; and on this oak
flooring lie the blue and scarlet patches from the stained west
window, more subduedly echoed in the velvets of the chair
coverings, the coloured marbles of the great Renaissance fireplace, and the fruits and garlands of the carved woodwork
surrounding the windows. There is nothing garish: all the
colours have melted into an old harmony that is one of the
principal beauties of these rooms. The walls here in the Cartoon Gallery are hung with rose-red Genoa velvet, so lovely
that I almost regret Mytens' copies of the Raphael cartoons
hiding most of it; but if, at Knole, one were too nicely reluctant to sacrifice the walls, whether panelled or velvet-hung,
then all the pictures would have to be stacked on the floor of
the attics. The same regret applies to the ball-room, where the
Elizabethan panelling—oak, but originally painted white,
turned by age to ivory—is so covered up as to be unnoticeable
behind the Sackville portraits of ten generations. Fortunately,
the frieze in the ball-room cannot be hidden. It used to delight

me as a child, with its carved intricacies of mermaids and dolphins, mermen and mermaids with scaly, twisting tails and salient anatomy, and I was invariably contemptuous of those visitors to whom I pointed out the frieze but who were more interested in the pictures. It always fell to my lot to "show the house" to visitors when I was there alone with my grandfather, for he shared the family failing of unsociability, and whenever a telegram arrived threatening invasion he used to take the next train to London for the day, returning in the evening when the coast was clear. It mattered nothing that I was every whit as bored by the invasion as he could have been; in a divergence between the wishes of eighty and the wishes of eight, the wishes of eight went to the wall.

The only other thing which took him to London was Mr. Willett's Daylight Saving Bill, introducing what we now call Summer Time. He never failed to go and vote for it in the House of Lords. I think it showed considerable imagination on Grandpapa's part, at his age, to realize a benefit which nearly everybody else was then opposing.

§ vi

There are other galleries, older and more austere than the Cartoon Gallery. They are not quite so long, they are narrower, lower, and darker, and not so exuberant in decoration; indeed, they are simply and soberly panelled in oak. They have the old, musty smell which, to me, wherever I met it, would bring back Knole. I suppose it is really the smell of all old houses— a mixture of woodwork, pot-pourri, leather, tapestry, and the little camphor bags which keep away the moth; the smell engendered by the shut windows of winter and the open windows of summer, with the breeze of summer blowing in from across the park. Bowls of lavender and dried rose-leaves stand on the window-sills; and if you stir them up you get the quintessence of the smell, a sort of dusty fragrance, sweeter in the under layers where it has held the damp of the spices. The pot-pourri at Knole is always made from the recipe of a prim-looking little lady who lived there for many years as a

uest in the reigns of George I and George II. Her two rooms
open out of one of the galleries, two of the smallest rooms in
the house, the bedroom hung with a pale landscape of blue-
green tapestry, the sitting-room panelled in oak; and in the
bedroom stands her small but pompous bed, with bunches of
ostrich-plumes nodding at each of the four corners. Strangers
usually seem to like these two little rooms best, coming to
them as they do, rather overawed by the splendour of the
galleries; they are amused by the smallness of the four-poster,
square as a box, its creamy lining so beautifully quilted; by
the spinning-wheel, with the shuttle still full of old flax; and
by the ring-box, containing a number of plain-cut stones,
which could be exchanged at will into the single gold setting
provided. The windows of these rooms, furthermore, look out
on to the garden; they are human, habitable little rooms,
reassuring after the pomp of the Ball-room and the galleries.
In the sitting-room there is a small portrait of the prim lady,
Lady Betty Germain, sitting very stiff in a blue brocaded
dress; she looks as though she had been a martinet in a tight,
narrow way.

The gallery leading to these rooms is called the Brown
Gallery. It is well named—oak floor, oak walls, and barrelled
ceiling, criss-crossed with oak slats in a pattern something
like cat's cradle. Some of the best pieces of the English furniture are ranged down each side of this gallery: portentously
important chairs, Jacobean cross-legged or later love-seats in
their original coverings, whether of plum and silver, or red
brocade with heavy fringes, or green with silver fringes, or
yellow silk sprigged in black, or powder-blue; and all have
their attendant stool squatting beside them. They are lovely,
silent rows, for ever holding out their arms, and for ever disappointed. At the end of this gallery is a tiny oratory, down
two steps, for the use of the devout: this little secret place
glows with colour like a jewel, but nobody ever notices it.
and on the whole it probably prefers to hide itself away
unobserved.

There is also the Leicester Gallery, which preserves in its
name the sole trace of Lord Leicester's brief ownership of

Knole. The Leicester Gallery is very dark and mysterious,
furnished with red velvet Cromwellian farthingale chairs and
sofas, dark as wine; there are illuminated scrolls of two family
pedigrees—Sackville and Curzon—richly emblazoned with
coats of arms, drawn out in 1589 and 1623 respectively; and
in the end window there is a small stained-glass portrait of
"Herbrand de Sackville, a Norman notable, came into England
with William the Conqueror, A.D. 1066." (*Herbrandus de
Sackville, Praepotens Normanus, intravit Angliam cum Gulielmo
Conquestore, Anno Domini MLXVI.*) There is also a curious
portrait hanging on one of the doors, of Catherine Fitzgerald,
Countess of Desmond, the portrait of a very old lady, in
black dress and a white ruff, with that strange far-away look
in her pale eyes that comes with extreme age. Bernhard
Berenson, somewhat to my surprise, once told me that in his
opinion it was by Rembrandt. Tradition says of her that she
was born in the reign of Edward the Fourth and died in
the reign of Charles the First, breaking her leg incidentally at
the age of ninety by falling off a cherry tree; that is to say
she was a child when the princes were smothered in the
Tower, a girl when Henry the Seventh came to the throne,
and watched the pageant of all the Tudors and the accession
of the Stuarts—the whole of English history enclosed between
the Wars of the Roses and the Civil War. She must have been
a truly legendary figure in the country by the time she had
reached the age of a hundred and forty or thereabouts.

It is rather a frightening portrait, that portrait of Lady
Desmond. If you go into the gallery after nightfall with a
candle the pale, far-away eyes stare past you into the dark
corners of the wainscot, eyes either over-charged or empty—
which? Knole is not haunted, but you require either an un-
imaginative nerve or else a complete certainty of the house's
benevolence before you can wander through the state-rooms
after nightfall with a candle, as I used to do when I was little.
There were no electric torches in those days. The light
gleamed on the dull gilding of furniture and into the misty
depths of mirrors, and started up a sudden face out of the
gloom; something creaked and sighed; the tapestry swayed

nd the figures on it undulated and seemed to come alive.
The recesses of the great beds, deep in shadow, might be inhabited, and you would not know what eyes might watch you,
unseen. The man with the candle is under a terrible disadvantage to the man in the dark. But I was never frightened
at Knole. I loved it; and took it for granted that Knole loved
me.

§ vii

As there are three galleries among the state-rooms, so are
here three principal bedrooms: the King's, the Venetian
Ambassador's, and the Spangled Room. The so-called King's
Bedroom has long been a subject of dispute. Fanny Burney,
writing to her sister Susanna in October 1779, remarks that
one of the state-rooms had been fitted up by an "Earle of
Dorsette for the bedchamber of King James I when upon a
visit to Knowle (*sic*); it had all the gloomy grandeur and
solemn finery of that time." Fanny Burney made a terrible
muddle over the state-bedrooms at Knole, and is a most un-
reliable witness. It was she who originated the tradition per-
petuated in my family that the King's Bedroom was prepared
for King James I. I used always meekly to repeat this legend,
but in wiser and better-informed years have come to the con-
clusion that it is without foundation. For one thing, there is
no mention of any visit to Knole in the detailed account of
the *Progresses of James I*. This, in itself, although negative,
would seem to be conclusive. Then, for the second thing,
there is the further indisputable contention that the sumptuous
character of the carving and upholstery suggests a later date,
more like Charles II than James I. I fear, therefore, that the
idea of James I ever laying his ugly head on those bumpily
embroidered pillows, or being enclosed within those coral-
coloured bed-curtains at night, must be forever discarded. I
am sorry about this, because the immense bed with its canopy
reaching almost to the ceiling, decked with ostrich feathers,
the hangings stiff with gold and silver thread, the coverlet and
the interior of the curtains heavily worked with a design of
pomegranates and tiger-lilies, the royal cipher embossed on

the pillows, should have been a bed for a King, even so unattractive and uninspiring a King as James I.

I don't know what else to say about the King's Bedroom, otherwise sometimes called the Silver Room. I know it is very famous, but I have never liked it, and it is no good writing a book like this unless one states one's own feelings and prejudices. I think it is the only vulgar room in the house. Not that the great bed is vulgar; that is magnificent in its way, and beautiful too. What is shockingly vulgar is the set of furniture made of embossed silver: the table, the hanging mirror, the tripods—all the florid and ostentatious product of the Restoration. Charles Sackville cannot have known when he had enough of a good thing. He did not have it all made for himself; the silver table, for instance, bears the initials in a monogram F.D.H.P. which can be interpreted as meaning Frances Dorset (Charles Sackville's mother) and Henry Powle, her second husband. It has been suggested that the silver furniture at Knole was copied from similar sets made for Louis XIV at Versailles, all of which was melted down to meet some of the expense of the wars against England. If this is true, the set at Knole would thus be the only reproduction still in existence.

There is a lot more silver in the King's Bedroom—there are silver sconces on the walls, ginger-jars, mirrors, fire-dogs, rose-water sprinklers, and a whole dressing-table set of hair-brushes and boxes, even to a little tiny eye-bath, all in silver. I often longed to brush my hair with what I wrongly supposed to be King James' brushes, but having been strictly brought up not to touch anything in the show-rooms I didn't dare.

It is almost a relief to go from here to the Venetian Ambassador's Bedroom. Green and gold; Burgundian tapestry, mediæval figures walking in a garden; a rosy Persian rug—of all rooms I never saw a room that so had over it a bloom like the bloom on a bowl of grapes and figs. I cannot keep the simile, which may convey nothing to those who have not seen the room, out of my mind. Greens and pinks originally bright, now dusted and tarnished over. It is a very grave, stately room, rather melancholy in spite of its stateliness. It seems to miss its inhabitants more than do any of the other rooms. Perhaps this is because the bed appears to be designed for three: it is of enormous breadth, and there are three pillows in a row. Presumably this is what the Italians call a *letto matrimoniale*.

§ viii

In a remote corner of the house is the Chapel of the Archbishops, small, and very much bejewelled. Tapestry, oak, and stained-glass—the chapel smoulders with colour. It is greatly improved since the oak has been pickled and the mustard-yellow paint removed, also the painted myrtle-wreaths, tied with a gilt ribbon, in the centre of each panel, with which the nineteenth century adorned it, when it was considered "very simple, plain, and neat in its appearance, and well adapted for family worship." The hand of the nineteenth century fell rather heavily on the chapel: besides painting the oak yellow and the ceiling blue with gold stars, it erected a Gothic screen and a yellow organ; but fortunately these are both at the entrance, and you can turn your back on them and look down the little nave to the altar where Mary Queen of Scots' gifts stand under the Perpendicular east window. All along the left-hand wall once hung the Gothic tapestry—scenes from the life of Christ, the figures, ungainly enough, trampling on an edging of tall irises and lilies exquisitely designed; and "Saint Luke in his first profession," wrote Horace Walpole irreverently, "holding a urinal." There used to be other tapestries in the house; there was one of the Seven Deadly Sins set, woven with gold threads, and there was another series, very early, representing the Flood and the two-by-two procession of the animals going into a weather-boarded Ark; but these, alas, had to be sold, and are now in America. So is the tapestry from the Chapel, which now hangs in the Museum at Boston, Massachusetts.

The chapel looks strange and lovely during a midnight thunderstorm: the lightning flashes through the stone ogives of the east window, and one gets a queer effect, unreal like colour photography, of the colours lit up by that unfamiliar means. A flight of little private steps leads out of my bedroom straight into the Family Pew; so I dare to say that there are few aspects under which I have not seen the chapel; and as a child I used to "take sanctuary" there when I had been naughty: that is to say, fairly often. They never found me sulking inside the pulpit. I used to think of John Donne, who sometimes preached there when he was Rector of Sevenoaks, reducing Lady Anne Clifford to tears.

§ ix

There would, of course, be many other aspects from which I might consider Knole; indeed, if I allowed myself full licence I might ramble out over Kent and down into Sussex, to Lewes, Buckhurst and Withyham, out into the fruit country and the hop country, across the Weald, over Saxonbury, and to Lewes among the Downs, and still I should not feel guilty of irrelevance. Of whatever English county I spoke, I still should be aware of the relationship between the English soil and that most English house. But more especially do I feel this concerning Kent and Sussex, and concerning the roads over which the Sackvilles travelled so constantly between estate and estate. The place-names in their letters recur through the centuries; the paper is a little yellower as the age increases, the ink a little more faded, the handwriting a little less easily decipherable, but still the gist is always the same: "I go to-morrow into Kent," "I quit Buckhurst for Knole," "my Lord rode to Lewes with a great company," "we came to Knole by coach at midnight." The whole district is littered with their associations, whether a village whose living lay in their gift, or a town where they endowed a college, or a wood where they hunted, or the village church where they had themselves buried. Sussex, in fact, was their cradle long before they came into Kent. Buckhurst, which they had owned since the twelfth century, was at one time an even larger house than Knole, and to their own vault in its parish church of Withyham they were invariably brought to rest. Their trace is scattered over the two counties. But this was not my only meaning; I had in mind that Knole was no mere excrescence, no alien fabrication, no startling stranger seen between the beeches and the oaks. No other country but England could have produced it, and into no other country would it settle with such harmony and such quiet. The very trees have not been banished from the courtyards, but spread their green against the stone. From the top of a tower one looks down upon the acreage of roofs, and the effect is less that of a palace than of a jumbled village upon the hillside. It is not an incongruity like Blenheim or Chatsworth, foreign to the spirit of England. It is, rather, the greater relation of those small manor-houses which hide themselves away so innumerably among the counties, whether built of the grey stone of southwestern England, or the brick of East Anglia, or merely tile-hung or plastered like the cottages. It is not utterly different from any of these. The great Palladian houses of the eighteenth century are *in* England, they are not *of* England, as are these irregular roofs, this easy straying up the contours of the hill, these cool coloured walls, these calm gables, and dark windows mirroring the sun.

CHAPTER II

THE GARDEN AND PARK

§ i

YOU COME out of the cool shadowy house on to the warm garden, in the summer, and there is a scared flutter of white pigeons up to the roof as you open the door. You have to look twice before you are sure whether they are pigeons or magnolias. The turf is of the most brilliant green; there is a sound of bees in the limes; the heat quivers like watered gauze above the ridge of the lawn. The garden is entirely enclosed by a high wall of rag, very massively built, and which perhaps dates back to the time of the archbishops or possibly built by the Lennards during their tenancy of Knole in 1565; its presence, I think, gives a curious sense of seclusion and quiet. Inside the walls are herbaceous borders on either side of long green walks, and little square orchards planted with very old apple-trees, under which grow iris, snapdragon, larkspur, pansies, and other humble flowers. There are also interior walls, with rounded archways through which one catches a sight of the house, so that the garden is conveniently divided up into sections without any loss of the homogeneity of the whole. Half of the garden, roughly speaking, is formal; the other half is woodland, called the Wilderness, mostly of beech and chestnut, threaded by mossy paths which in spring are thick with bluebells and daffodils.

The old engravings show the gardens to have been, from the seventeenth century onwards, very much the same as they are at present. There are a few minor variations, but as the early engravers were not very particular as to accuracy their evidence cannot be accepted as wholly reliable. We have, besides these engravings, a fairly large number of records relating to both the park and gardens. The earliest of these that I have been able to trace is dated 1456, to the effect that Archbishop Bourchier in that year enclosed the park—a

smaller area then than is covered by it now; and in 1468 there
is a bill, "Paid for making 1000 palings for the enclosure of
the Knole land, 6s. 8d." But the first accounts for the garden
proper appear to date from the reign of Henry VIII (State
papers of Henry VIII), when, in 1543, Sir Richard Longe was
paid "for making the King's garden at Knole." Then there
is a gap of nearly a century, save for the references to the
garden in Lady Anne Clifford's Diary, such as "25th October,
1617. My Lady Lisle and my Coz: Barbara Sidney [came?]
and I walked with them all the Wilderness over. They saw the
Child and much commended her. I gave them some marma-
lade of quince, for about this time I made much of it"; and
her constant notes of how she took her prayer-book "up to
the standing" [which I take to be what we now call the
Duchess' Seat], or of how she picked cherries in the garden
with the French page, and he told her how he thought that all
the men in the house loved her. For the year 1692, however,
there are some bills among the Knole papers, such as "Mr.
Olloynes, gardener, wages £12 per annum," and some bills
for seeds and roots, "Sweet yerbs, pawsley, sorrill, spinnig,
spruts, leeks, sallet, horse-rydish, jerusalem hawty-chorks,"
and another bill for seeds for £2 0s. 5d. Coming to the eighteenth century, there are more detailed accounts, amongst
others an agreement of what was expected in those days of a
head gardener and the remuneration he might hope to receive:

14th Aug., 1706. Ric. Baker, Gardener with Lionel Earl of
Dorset and Middlesex. To serve his Lordship as Gardener
at Knole for the term of one year ½ to begin in March 1706.
That he will reserve all the fruit which shall be growing in the
garden for his Lordship's use. That he will at his own charge
during the said term preserve all Trees and Greens now in
the garden, and will maintain the trees in good husbandlike
manner by pruning and trimming, dunging and marling the
same in seasonable times, and likewise at his own charge will
provide all herbs and other things convenient for my Lord's
kitchen there when in season. He undertakes to maintain at
his own charge all such walks as are now in ye said Garden,
by mowing, cleaning, and rolling the same, and will preserve

all such flowers and plants as are now in the gardens, and that he will be at all the charges of repairing all the glass frames, etc. belonging to the Garden Trade, and will provide for the present use of the Gardens 50 loads of dung.

In return for this service he was to be allowed £30 per annum, and

rooms and conveniences in the house for his business, and to hand all such dung, etc. as shall be made about the house for the use of ye gardens, and that he may have the privilege of disposing [for his own use] all such beans, peas, cabbages, and other kitchen herbs as shall be spared, over and above that what is used in my Lord's kitchen.

	£	s.	d.
April 28, 1718.			
Planting trees in new Oak Walk, 5 men, 8 to 18 days each	3	12	4
Planting walnut trees round the Keeper's lodge, 3 men, 5 days each at 1/2 each per day	0	17	6
Cutting Bows in the yew at end of new Oak Walk	0	2	4
November 11, 1723.			
Cutting and levelling new walk in ye Wilderness and making ye mount round ye Oak tree, 8 men, 5 to 11 days each	3	10	0
Alterations made in the Fruit Walks, 16 men, from 14 to 43 days each	23	19	10
Cutting 10,600 turfs at 8d. per 100	3	10	8
Planting ye quarry in the Park	6	7	0
10 May Duke Cherries in ye garden	0	6	8
6 peach and nectarine trees in ye garden	0	12	0
2400 quick-set for ye kitchen garden	0	12	0
1000 holly for ye kitchen garden	0	10	0
Planting 2000 small beeches in ye park	0	18	6
200 Pear stocks	0	6	0
300 Crab stocks	0	3	0
200 Cherry stocks	0	6	0
500 Holly stocks	0	5	0
700 Hazel stocks	1	15	0

	£	s.	d.
November 11, 1723.			
For new making the Mulberry garden and sowing ye front walk with seed	14	12	9
200 Gascon Cherry trees	0	10	0
50 bushels sweet apples for cyder	2	10	0
1 bushel Buckwheat for ye Pheasants	0	3	6
10,000 seedling beeches for my Lady Germaine	0	10	0
December 24, 1726.			
Getting 80 load of ice and putting it in ye Ice House	1	15	3
June 15, 1728.			
Planting 160 Elms in field which was Dr. Lambarde's next Tonbridge road and sowing the field with furze seed	7	9	3
April, 1730.			
1000 Asparagus plants from Gravesend	1	0	0
2 doz. Apricots	0	2	0
300 beeches 8 ft. high	1	15	0
250 large beeches planted in ye Park	3	10	0

It is not very clear where such a large number of fruit trees were to be used, but on an engraving of about 1720 I find a wall extending right across the garden to the two stone pillars which, surmounted by carved stone urns, still remain, this wall being planted with fruit trees, so I should think it very probable that this would account for it.

In 1777 new hot-houses and "Pineries" were built, and £175 paid for "two hot-houses full stocked with pine apples and plants."

§ ii

Surrounding the house and gardens lies the park, with its valleys, hills, and woods, and its short brown turf closely bitten by deer and rabbits. Its beeches and bracken, its glades and valleys, greatly excited the admiration of Mrs. Ann Radcliffe, who visited it in the beginning of the nineteenth century, and wrote with enthusiasm of shade rising above shade with

amazing and *magnificent* grandeur, and of one beech in particular spreading "its light yet umbrageous fan" over a seat
placed round the bole. With all its grandeur and luxuriance,
she said, there was nothing about this beech heavy or formal;
it was airy, though vast and majestic, and suggested an idea
at once of the *strength* and *fire* of a *hero*. She would call a beech
tree, and this beech above every other, the hero of the forest,
as the oak was called the king.

As I have said, the park was first enclosed by Bourchier in
1456, the year in which he bought Knole on the 30th of June.
In the muniments at Lambeth are a number of papers relating
to the expenses of this great builder, and there is the interesting fact that glass-making was carried on in the park, and I
only wish that more detailed accounts existed of this industry,
which, thanks to the Huguenots, had been pretty widely introduced into the South of England. I should like to know
exactly where their glass-foundry was, and whether they
made use of the sand on the portion known as the Furze-field,
now a rabbit-warren; and I should also very much like to
know whether—as seems probable—they supplied any of the
glass for the windows in the house.

It would appear that the park, now entirely under grass,
was once ploughland, for there is at Knole a deed of the time
of Richard Sackville, fifth Earl of Dorset—that is to say, the
middle of the seventeenth century—which accords to four
farmers "the liberty to plough anywhere in the Park except
in the plain set out by my Lord and the ground in front of the
house, and to take three crops, and it is agreed that one-third
of each crop after it is severed from the ground shall be taken
and carried away by my Lord for his own use. The third year,
the farmers to sow the ground with grass seed if my Lord
desires it, and they are to be at the charge of the seed, the
tillage, and the harvest." Later on, in the time of Charles I,
hops were grown, not only around the park, but also in it.
Women employed in picking the hops were paid 5*d*. a day,
but for cleaning and weeding the ground they only received
3*d*. At this time also cattle were fed in the park during the
summer, and belonging to the same date (about 1628) are the

bills for "Moles caught, $1\frac{1}{2}d$. each"; "Mowing the meadows," at the rate of $1s$. $6d$. per acre; "Making hay," also at $1s$. $6d$. per acre; "Carriage of hay from the meadows to Knole barn," $1s$. $4d$. per load: "one hay fork and 2 hay forks together," $1s$. $8d$. For "hunting conies by night and ferret by day" $4s$. was paid; the expenses involved by the "conies" for one year were exactly £10, which included £5 $5s$., a year's wages for the "wariner"; but, on the other hand, this was money well expended, for the revenue from "conies sold" covers no less than a fifth part of the year's total income. The "wariner", although his £5 $5s$. a year hardly seems excessive, did better than the "wood-looker," who, for his woodreeveship for a year, was paid only £2.

The accounts of how and when the various outlying portions of the park were taken in can only be of local interest, and I do not therefore propose to go into them. They were mostly bought by John Frederick, the third duke, and by Lord Whitworth, who had married John Frederick's widow. The ruins round the queer little sham Gothic house called the Bird House—which always frightened me as a child because I thought it looked like the witch's house in Hansel and Gretel, tucked away in its hollow, with its pointed gables— were built for John Frederick's grandfather about 1761, by one Captain Robert Smith, who had fought at Minden under Lord George Sackville, of disastrous notoriety, and who lived for some time at Knole, a parasite upon the house; they apparently purport to be the remains of some vast house, in defiance of the fact that no upper storey or roof of proportionate dimensions could ever possibly have rested upon the flimsy structure of flint and rubble which constitute the ruins. They, together with the Bird House, form an amusing group of the whims and vanities of two different ages. But, to go back to the park, I conclude with the following letter, which is among the papers at Knole:

To his Grace the DUKE *of* DORSET.

My Lord,
      I Elizabeth Hills sister and executor of Mrs Anne Hills

deceased of Under River in the Parish of Seal and whose corpse is to be interred in the Parish Church of Seal: but the High Road leading thereto by Golden Green being very bad and unsafe for carriages: I beg leave of yr Grace to permit the proper attendants to pass with the corpse, in a hearse with the coaches in attendance through Knole Park: entering the same at Faulke [*sic*] Common Gate and going out at the gate at Lock's Bottom: and you'll oblige

Your Grace's most obedient serv^t

UNDER RIVER,   ELIZA HILLS.

    18 *Oct.*, 1781.

§ iii

So much, then, for the setting; but it is no mere empty scene. The house, with its exits and entrances, its properties of furniture and necessities, its dressing-tables, its warming-pans, and its tiny silver eye-bath still standing between the hair-brushes—the house demands its population. Whose were the hands that have, by the constant light running of their fingers, polished the paint from the banisters? Whose were the feet that have worn down the flags of the hall and the stone passages? What child rode upon the ungainly rocking-horse? What young men exercised their muscles on the ropes of the great dumb-bell? Who were the men and women that, after a day's riding or stitching, lay awake in the deep beds, idly watching between the curtains the play of the firelight, and the little round yellow discs cast upon walls and ceiling through the perforations of the tin canisters standing on the floor, containing the rush-lights?

Thus the house wakes into a whispering life, and we resurrect the Sackvilles.

CHAPTER III

KNOLE IN THE REIGN OF QUEEN ELIZABETH

THOMAS SACKVILLE, Lord Buckhurst *and* 1st Earl *of* Dorset

§ i

SUCH interest as the Sackvilles have lies, I think, in their being so representative. From generation to generation they might stand, fully equipped, as portraits from English history. Unless they are to be considered in this light they lose their purport; they merely share, as Byron wrote to one of their number:

> . . . . *with titled crowds the common lot,*
> *In life just gazed at, in the grave forgot . . .*
> *The mouldering 'scutcheon, or the herald's roll,*
> *That well-emblazoned but neglected scroll,*
> *Where lords, unhonoured, in the tomb may find*
> *One spot, to leave a worthless name behind:*
> *There sleep, unnoticed as the gloomy vaults*
> *That veil their dust, their follies, and their faults:*
> *A race with old armorial lists o'erspread*
> *In records destined never to be read.*

But let them stand each as the prototype of his age, and at the same time as a link to carry on, not only the tradition but also the heredity of his race, and they immediately acquire a significance, a unity. You have first the grave Elizabethan, with the long, rather melancholy face, emerging from the oval frame above the black clothes and the white wand of office; you perceive all his severe integrity; you understand the intimidating austerity of the contribution he made to English letters. Undoubtedly a fine old man. You come down to his grandson: he is the Cavalier by Vandyck hanging in the hall, hand on hip, his flame-coloured doublet slashed across by the blue of the Garter; this is the man who raised a troop of horse off his own estates and vowed never to cross the threshold of his

house into an England governed by the murderers of the
King. You have next the florid, magnificent Charles, the fruit
of the Restoration, poet, and patron of poets, prodigal, jovial
and licentious; you have him full-length, by Sir Geoffrey
Kneller, in his Garter robes and his enormous wig, his foot
and fine calf well thrust forward; you have him less pompous
and more intimate, wrapped in a dressing-gown of figured
silk, the wig replaced by an Hogarthian turban; but it is still
the same coarse face, with the heavy jowl and the twinkling
eyes, the crony of Rochester and Sedley, the patron and host
of Pope and Dryden, Prior and Killigrew. You come down to
the eighteenth century. You have on Gainsborough's canvas
the beautiful, sensitive face of the gay and fickle duke, spoilt,
feared, and propitiated by the women of London and Paris,
the reputed lover of Marie Antoinette. You have his son, too,
fair and pretty a boy, the friend of Byron, killed in the hunting
field at the age of twenty-one, the last direct male of a race
too prodigal, too amorous, too weak, too indolent, and too
melancholy.

§ ii

The Sackvilles are supposed to have gone into Normandy
in the ninth century with Rollo the Dane, and to have settled
in the neighbourhood of Dieppe, in a small town called Sal-
cavilla, from which, obviously, they derived their name. Much
as I relish the suggestion of this Norse origin, I am bound to
add that the first of whom there is any authentic record is
Herbrand de Sackville, contemporary with William the Conqueror, whom he accompanied to England. Descending from
him is a long monotonous list of Sir Jordans, Sir Andrews,
Sir Edwards, Sir Richards, carrying us through the Crusades,
the French wars, and the wars of the Roses, but none of whom
has the slightest interest until we get to Sir Richard Sackville,
temp. Henry VIII–Elizabeth—from his wealth called Sackfill
or Fillsack, though not, it appears, "either griping or penur-
ious," a man of some note, and thus qualified by Roger
Ascham: "That worthy gentleman, that earnest favourer and
furtherer of God's true religion; that faithful servitor to his

rince and country; a lover of learning and all learned men; ise in all doings; courteous to all persons, showing spite to one, doing good to many; and, as I well found, to me so fast friend as I never lost the like before"; and in this same conection I may quote further from Ascham's preface to *The cholemaster*, in which he records a conversation which took lace in 1593 between himself and Sir Richard Sackville, when ining with Sir William Cecil: Sir Richard, after complaining f his own education by a bad schoolmaster, said, "But seeing is but in vain to lament things past, and also wisdom to look things to come, surely, God willing (if God lend me life), I ill make this my mishap some occasion of good hap to little Robert Sackville, my son's son; for whose bringing up I would ladly, if so please you, use specially your good advice." . . . I wish also," says Ascham, "with all my heart, that young Mr. Robert Sackville may take that fruit of this labour that is worthy grandfather purposed he should have done. And f any other do take profit or pleasure hereby, they have cause thank Mr. Robert Sackville, for whom specially this my cholemaster was provided."

This Sir Richard was the founder of the family fortune, which was to be increased by his son and squandered after hat by nearly all his decendants in succession. It was he who ought, in 1564, for the sum of £641 5s. 10½d., "the whole of he land lying between Bridewell and Water Lane from Fleet Street to the Thames." This property, now of course of almost abulous value, included the house then known as Salisbury House, having belonged to the see of Salisbury, which resently became Dorset House in 1603, and presently again vas divided into Great Dorset House and Little Dorset House, s the London house of the Sackvilles. A wall enclosed house nd gardens from the existing line of Salisbury Court south the river, and shops and tenements in and near Fleet Street rom St. Bride's to Water Lane (Whitefriars Street). These vere not the only London possessions of the Sackvilles. Later n they overflowed into the Strand, and another Dorset House sprang up, on the site of the present Treasury in Whitehall, to take the place of the older house in Salisbury

Court, which had been destroyed in the Great Fire. It is id
and exasperating to speculate on the modern value of thes
City estates.

Sir Richard Sackville died in 1566, when his son Thoma
was already thirty years of age. Very little is known abou
Thomas' early life; we only know that he went for a sho
time to Oxford (Hertford), and subsequently to the Inne
Temple. While at Oxford he attracted some attention as
poet and writer of sonnets; but I have only been able to fin
one of these early sonnets, written for Hoby's translation o
the *Courtier of Count Baldessar Castilio* (published in 1561
and which I quote, not so much for its worth as for its intere
as a little-known work from the pen of one who, as the autho
of our earliest tragedy, has a certain renown:

> *These royal Kings, that rear up to the sky*
> *Their palace tops, and deck them all with gold:*
> *With rare and curious works they feed the eye,*
> *And show what riches here great princes hold.*
> *A rarer work, and richer far in worth,*
> *Castilio's hand presenteth here to thee:*
> *No proud nor golden court doth he set forth*
> *But what in court a courtier ought to be.*
> *The prince he raiseth huge and mighty walls,*
> *Castilio frames a wight of noble fame:*
> *The King with gorgeous tissue clads his halls,*
> *The court with golden virtue decks the same*
> *Whose passing skill, lo, Hoby's pen displays*
> *To Britain folk a work of worthy praise.*

But for the rest concerning these early poems one mus
take his contemporary Jasper Heywood's eulogy on trust:

> *There Sackville's sonnets sweetly sauced*
> *And featly finèd be.*

It seems that Sackville's works were all written in the firs
half of his life, and that later on, as honours came to him, h
altogether abandoned what might have been a first-rat
literary career for a second-rate political one—more's th

ity. "A born poet," says Mr. Gosse, "diverted from poetry by the pursuits of statesmanship." He is a very good instance of the disadvantage of fine birth to a poet. But for the fact that he was born the Queen's cousin, through the Boleyns, and the son of a father holding various distinguished offices, he might never have entered a political arena where he was destined to have as competitors such statesmen as Burleigh, and such favourites as Leicester and Essex. Amongst his contemporary poets, Surrey and Wyatt both died while Sackville was still a child; when Spenser was born, Sackville was already sixteen; when Sidney was born, he was eighteen; when Shakespeare was born, he was a full-grown man of twenty-eight. He had thus the good fortune to be born at a time when English poets of much standing were rare, an opportunity of which he might have taken greater advantage had not the accident of his birth persuaded him to abandon poetry for more serious things as the dilettantism of his youth. For he was comparatively young when he wrote both *Gorboduc* and the *Induction* to the *Mirror for Magistrates*. *Gorboduc* was first performed by the gentlemen of the Inner Temple before the Queen in 1561, when Sackville was twenty-five, and the *Induction* was first published in 1563, when he was twenty-seven; but already in or about 1557, when he was only just over twenty, he had composed the plan for the whole of the *Mirror for Magistrates*, intending to write it himself, although subsequently from want of leisure he left the composition of all but the induction or introduction, and the *Complaint of Henry, Duke of Buckingham*, to others.

By the age of twenty-one, however, responsibilities were already upon him. He was married; and he was a member of Parliament, not merely once but twice over, as appears from the journals of the House of Commons: "For that Thomas Sackville, Esq., is returned for the County of Westmoreland, and also for the Borough of East Grinstead in Sussex, and doth personally appear for Westmoreland, it is required by this House that another person be returned for the said borough." How this double election can have come about I cannot explain. It seems to have done him no harm in his

parliamentary career; not only was he returned member fo
Aylesbury in 1563, but he took an active part in introducing
bills, etc. About this time he went to travel in France and
Italy, where for some mysterious reason he got himself thrown
into prison; the reason was probably pecuniary, for we are told
that he was "of the height of spirit inherent in his house,"
and lived too magnificently for his means; so I think the
assumption is in favour of his having got temporarily into
debt. If, indeed, he shared in any measure the tastes of his
descendants, nothing is more likely. Back in England again,
the successes of his career rushed upon him. His father was
just dead; he was the head of his family; he inherited its
wealth and estates; he was at the propitious age of thirty; he
was related to the Queen; he was marked out to prosper.
Within the next thirty years or so he was, successively
knighted and created Lord Buckhurst of Buckhurst, in the
county of Sussex; given the house and lands of Knole by the
Queen, that she might have him near her court and councils;
sent to France and the Netherlands as special ambassador from
Elizabeth; made a Knight of the Garter; Chancellor of Oxford,
where he sumptuously entertained the Queen; made Lord
High Treasurer of England in 1599; High Steward of England
at the trial of Essex, where he sat in state under a canopy and
pronounced sentence and an exhortation, says Bacon, "with
gravity and solemnity." By this time, I imagine, he had in very
truth became the grave and solemn personage one sees in all
his portraits—not that his mind, even in early youth, can
have been otherwise than grave and solemn if at the age of
twenty he had been capable of imagining a vast poem on so
dreary and Dantesque a plan as the *Mirror for Magistrates*,
devised, says Morley in his *English Literature*, "to moralise
those incidents of English history which warn the powerful of
the unsteadiness of fortune by showing them, as in a mirror,
that 'who reckless rules, right soon may hap to rue.'" Also,
from a letter written by Lord Buckhurst to Lord Walsingham,
it is clear that he had no sympathy with ostentation, but only
with honest worth: "And, Sir, I beseech you send over as few
Court captains as may be; but that they may rather be fur-

ished with captains here [in the Low Countries], such as by heir worthiness and long service do merit it, and do further eek to shine in the field with virtue and valiance against the nemy than with gold lace and gay garments in Court at ome." In 1586 Lord Buckhurst was one of the forty appointed on the commission for the trial of Mary Stuart, and although his name is not amongst those who proceeded to Fotheringay, nor later in the Star Chamber at Westminster when she was condemned to death, yet he was sent to announce the sentence to death, and received from her in recognition of his tact and gentleness in conveying this news the triptych and carved group of the Procession to Calvary now on the altar in the chapel at Knole.

He was, in fact, absent from none of the councils of the nation, and I have no doubt that he discharged his duties with all seriousness and honesty. Poetry—a frivolous pursuit—had long since been left behind. The poet had become the statesman. Nevertheless there were times when his very integrity was the cause of bringing him into disfavour with the intolerant mistress he served, notably on one occasion when he refused to take the part of Leicester and was indignantly confined to his house for nine or ten months by Royal mandate. And there was another occasion, amusing as showing the extreme simplicity in which even a man like Lord Buckhurst, who had the reputation of lavish living in his own day, conducted his daily life. Buckhurst, then being at the royal palace of Shene, was desired by the Queen to entertain Odet de Coligny, Cardinal of Chatillon, and did so, but with the result made clear in the following letter, of which I give extracts:

To the Right Honourable the Lords of her Majesty's Privy Council be this delivered.

My duty to your Lordships most humbly remembered.
Returning yesterday to Shene, I received as from your Lordships how her highness stood greatly displeased with me, for that I had not in better sort entertained the Cardinal.

He goes on to speak of his "great grief" and his "sorrowful heart," especially, he says, "being to her Majesty as I am," and proceeds with the attempt to justify himself for his supposed niggardliness:

I brought them in to every part of the house that I possessed, and showed them all such stuff and furniture as I had. And where they required plate of me, I told them as troth is, that I had no plate at all. Such glass vessel as I had I offered them, which they thought too base; for napery I could not satisfy their turn, for they desired damask work for a long table, and I had none other but plain linen for a square table. The table whereon I dine myself I offered them, and for that it was a square table they refused it. One only tester and bedstead not occupied I had, and those I delivered for the Cardinal himself, and when we could not by any means in so short a time procure another bedstead for the Bishop, I assigned them the bedstead on which my wife's waiting women did lie, and laid them on the ground. Mine own basin and ewer I lent to the Cardinal and wanted myself. So did I the candlesticks for mine own table, with divers drinking glasses, small cushions, small pots for the kitchen, and sundry other such like trifles, although indeed I had no greater store of them than I presently occupied; and albiet this be not worthy the writing, yet mistrusting lest the misorder of some others in denying of such like kind of stuff not occupied by themselves, have been percase informed as towards me, I have thought good not to omit it. Long tables, forms, brass for the kitchen, and all such necessaries as could not be furnished by me, we took order to provide in the town; hangings and beds we received from the yeoman of the wardrobe at Richmond, and when we saw that napery and sheets could nowhere here be had, I sent word thereof to the officers at the Court, by which means we received from my lord of Leicester 2 pair of fine sheets for the Cardinal, and from my lord Chamberlain one pair of fine for the bishop, with 2 other coarser pair, and order beside for 10 pair more from London.

At which time also because I would be sure your Lordships should be ascertained of the simpleness and scarcity of such stuff as I had here, I sent a man of mine to the Court, specially to declare to your Lordships that for plate, damask, napery and fine sheets, I had none at all and for the rest of my stuff neither was it such as with honour might furnish such a personage, nor yet had I any greater store thereof than I presently occupied, and he brought me this answer again from your Lordships that if I had it not I could not lend it. And yet all things being thus provided for, and the diet for his Lordship being also prepared, I sent word thereof to Mr. Kingesmele and thereupon the next day in the morning about nine of the clock the Cardinal came to Shene where I met and received him almost a quarter of a mile from the house, and when I had first brought the Cardinal to his lodging, and after the bishop to his, I thought good there to leave them to their repose. Thus having accommodated his Lordship as well as might be with so short a warning, I thought myself to have fully performed the meaning of your Lordships' letters unto me, and because I had tidings the day before that a house of mine in the country by sudden chance was burned . . . I took horse and rode the same night towards those places, where I found so much of my house burned as 200 marks will not repair . . .

This is not at all in accordance with his reputation for hospitality:

He kept house for forty and two years in an honourable proportion. For thirty years of these his family consisted of little less, in one place or another, than two hundred persons. But for more than twenty years, besides workmen and other hired, his number at the least hath been two hundred and twenty daily, as appeared upon check-role. A very rare example in this present age of ours, when housekeeping is so decayed.

I think that this reputation, and the enormous sums which he spent upon the enlargement and beautifying of Knole, make all the more remarkable the statements in the foregoing letter: that he had neither napery, plate, nor sheets, and that in order to provide his guest with a basin and ewer he was obliged to do without them himself. It is apparent also from his will that he indulged himself in the luxury of various musicians, "some for the voice and some for the instrument, whom I have found to be honest in their behaviour and skilful in their profession, and who had often given me after the labour and painful travels of the day much recreation and contatation with

their delightful harmony." "Musicians," it was said, "th
most curious he could have," so that in these extravagance
he was not parsimonious, although he disregarded the commo
comforts of life.

In June 1566 Queen Elizabeth had presented him wit
Knole, but, because the house was then both let and sub-let
it was not until 1603 that he was able to take possession
Tradition says that the Queen bestowed Knole upon hin
because she wished to have him nearer to her court ane
councils, and to spare him the constant journey betwee
London and Buckhurst, over the rough, clay-sodden roads o
the Weald, at that date still an uncultivated and almost un
inhabited district, where droves of wild swine rootled fo
acorns under the oaks. He does not appear to have spent very
much time at Knole during the first years of his ownership
for in a letter written in September 1605, to Lord Salisbury
he says: "I go now to Horsley, and thence to Knole, where
was not but once in the first beginnings all the year, whenc
for three or four days to Buckhurst, where I was not thes
seven years." This did not prevent him from spending a grea
deal of money on the house; unfortunately there is no recorc
of what he spent between 1603 and 1607, but for the last te
months of his life alone there is a total, spent on buildings
material, and stock, for four thousand one hundred and sever
pounds, eleven shillings, and ninepence—an equivalent, i
round figures, to forty thousand of modern money. To ac
count for these sums, it is known that he built the Grea
Staircase, transformed the Great Hall to its present state, anc
put in the plaster-work ceilings and marble chimney-pieces
He also put up the very lovely lead water-spouts in the
courtyards.

The good fortune of Lord Buckhurst did not come to ar
end with the death of Queen Elizabeth. He was one of those
who travelled to meet the new King on his journey down fron
the North, was confirmed by him in his tenure of the office o
Lord Treasurer, and early in the following year was createc
Earl of Dorset. The illuminated patents of creation are a
Knole, showing portraits of both Elizabeth and James I, no

very flattering to either; and the Lord Treasurer's chest is a Knole likewise, a huge coffer covered in leather and thickly studded with large round-headed brass nails. There is a warrant, signed by him as Lord Treasurer, for increasing the duty on tobacco, "That tobacco, being a drug brought into England of late years in small quantities, was used and taken by the better sort only as physic to preserve health; but through evil custom and the toleration thereof that riotous and disorderly persons spent most of their time in that idle vanity." This warrant, which is dated 1605, shows how little time had elapsed since its introduction before tobacco established its popularity.

He was now advancing in years, and his own letters prove that his health was not very good. In one letter, written to Cecil, he complains that he cannot rest more than two or three hours in the night at most, also that he is constantly subject to rheums and cold and coughs, forced to defend himself with warmth, and to fly the air in cold or moist weathers. In another letter, also written to Cecil, he again complains of a cough, and says that he cannot come abroad for three or four days at least. But his devotion to his public affairs was greater than his attention to his health, for he says, "I have by the space of this month and more foreborne to take physic by reason of her Majesty's business, and now having this only week left for physic I am resolved to prevent sickness, feeling myself altogether distempered and filled with humours, so as if her Majesty should miss me I beseech you in respect hereof to excuse me." In 1607, when the old man was seventy-one, there was a report current in London that he was dead, but on the King sending him a diamond, and wishing that he might live so long as that ring would continue, "My Lord Treasurer," says a letter dated June 1607, "revived again." In the following year, however, he died dramatically in harness, of apoplexy while sitting at the Council table in Whitehall. His funeral service took place in Westminster Abbey, but his body was taken to Withyham, where it now lies buried in the vault of his ancestors.

§ iii

I have dealt as briefly as possible with the Lord Treasurer's life, because no one could pretend that the history of his embassies or his occupations of office could have any interest save to a student of the age of Elizabeth. But as a too-much-neglected poet I should like presently to quote the opinions of those well qualified to judge, showing that he was, at least something of a pioneer in English literature—crude, of course, and uniformly gloomy; too gloomy to read, save as a labour of love or conscience; but nevertheless the author—or part-author—of the earliest English tragedy, and, in some passages, a poet of a certain sombre splendour. That he was a true poet, I think, is unquestionable, unlike his descendant Charles, who by virtue of one song in particular continues to survive in anthologies, but who was probably driven into verse by the fashion of his age rather than by any genuine urgency of creation.

The tragedy of *Gorboduc*, whose title was afterwards altered to *Ferrex and Porrex*, was written in collaboration with Thomas Norton, although the exact share of each author is not precisely known and has been much argued.

To the modern reader [says Professor Saintsbury] *Gorboduc* is scarcely inviting, but that is not a condition of its attractiveness to its own contemporaries. [It] is of the most painful regularity; and the scrupulosity with which each of the rival princes is provided with a counsellor and a parasite to himself, and the other parts are allotted with similar fairness, reaches such a point that it is rather surprising that *Gorboduc* was not provided with two queens—a good and a bad. But even these faults are perhaps less trying to the modern reader than the inchoate and unpolished condition of the metre in the choruses, and indeed in the blank verse dialogue. Here and there there are signs of the stateliness and poetical imagery of the *Induction*, but for the most part the decasyllables stop dead at their close and begin afresh at their beginning with a staccato movement and a dull monotony of cadence which is inexpressibly tedious.

Professor Saintsbury rightly points out that the dullness of *Gorboduc* to our ideas is not a criterion of the effect it produced on readers of its own day. Sir Philip Sidney, for example, while excepting it from the particular charges he brings against all other English tragedies and comedies, and granting that "it is full of stately speeches and well-sounding phrases, climbing to the height of Seneca his style, and as full of notable morality, which it doth most delightfully teach, and so obtain the very end of poesy," finds fault with it in an unexpected quarter, namely, that it fails in two unities, of time and place, so that the modern criticism of its "painful regularity" was far from occurring to a mind intent upon a yet more rigorous form.

In spite of its manifest imperfections [says the Cambridge Modern History], the tragedy of *Gorboduc* has two supreme claims to honourable commemoration. It introduced Englishmen who knew no language but their own to an artistic conception of tragedy, and it revealed to them the true mode of tragic expression.

I might also quote here the sonnet of a greater poet, who owed much, if not to *Gorboduc*, at least to the *Induction*— Edmund Spenser.

> *In vain I think, right honourable lord,*
> *By this rude rhyme to memorize thy name,*
> *Whose learnèd muse hath writ her own record*
> *In golden verse worthy immortal fame.*
> *Thou much more fit (were leisure to the same)*
> *Thy gracious sovereign's praises to compile,*
> *And her imperial majesty to frame*
> *In lofty numbers and heroic style.*
> *But sith thou may'st not so, give leave awhile*
> *To baser wit his power therein to spend,*
> *Whose gross defaults thy dainty pen may file,*
> *And unadvisèd oversights amend.*
> *But evermore vouchsafe it to maintain*
> *Against vile Zoylus' backbitings vain.*

There is also a sonnet by Joshua Sylvester, of which I will only quote the anagram prefixed to it:

Sackvilus   Comes Dorsetius
Vas Lucis   *Esto decor Musis*
       Sacris Musis celo devotus

But although there can scarcely be two opinions about *Gorboduc*—that it is sometimes noble, and always dull—Sackville's two other poems, the *Induction* to the *Mirror for Magistrates* and the *Complaint of Henry Duke of Buckingham*, have never met with the recognition they deserve, save for the discriminating applause of men of letters. I do not say that they are works which can be read through with an unvarying degree of pleasure; there are stagnant passages which have to be waded through in between the more admirable portions. But such portions, when they are reached, do contain much of the genuine stuff of poetry, impressive imagery, a surprising absence of cumbersome expression—especially when the reader bears in mind that Sackville was writing before Spenser, and long before Marlowe—and a diction which is consistently dignified and suitable to the gravity of the theme. Take these stanzas for instance:

> *And first within the porch and jaws of hell*
> *Sat deep* Remorse of Conscience, *all besprent*
> *With tears; and to herself oft would she tell*
> *Her wretchedness, and cursing never stent*
> *To sob and sigh; but ever thus lament,*
>   *With thoughtful care, as she that, all in vain,*
>   *Would wear and waste continually in pain.*

> *Next saw we* Dread, *all trembling: how he shook*
> *With foot uncertain, proffered here and there,*
> *Benumbed of speech, and, with a ghastly look,*
> *Searched every place, all pale and dead for fear,*
> *His cap borne up with staring of his hair,*
>   *'Stoin'd and amazed at his own shade for dread*
>   *And fearing greater dangers than he need.*

And next, in order sad, Old Age we found,
His beard all hoar, his eyes hollow and blind,
With drooping cheer still poring on the ground,
As on the place where Nature him assigned
To rest, when that the sisters had untwined
  His vital thread, and ended with their knife
  The fleeting course of fast-declining life.

These stanzas are from the *Induction*. Or take the following from the *Complaint of the Duke of Buckingham*:

Midnight was come, and every vital thing
With sweet sound sleep their weary limbs did rest;
The beasts were still, the little birds that sing
Now sweetly slept beside their mother's breast,
The old and all well shrouded in their nest;
  The waters calm, the cruel seas did cease,
  The woods, the fields, and all things held their peace.

The golden stars were whirled amid their race,
And on the earth did with their twinkling light,
When each thing nestled in his resting place,
Forget day's pain with pleasure of the night;
  The fearful deer of death stood not in doubt,
  The partridge dreamt not of the falcon's foot.

These quotations will give some kind of idea of Sackville's matter and manner, and of the *Mirror*, which survives among the classic monuments of English poetry, says Courthope, only by virtue of the genius of Sackville. For the rest, not wishing to be thought prejudiced, I should like to quote copiously from Professor Saintsbury's *Elizabethan Literature*, since therein is expressed, a great deal better than I could express it, my own view of Sackville's poetry, and by calling in the testimony of so excellent, scholarly, and delightful an authority I may be freed from the charge of partiality which I should not at all like to incur.

The next remarkable piece of work done in English poetry after Tottel's *Miscellany*—a piece of work of greater actual

poetic merit than anything in the *Miscellany* itself—was . .
the famous *Mirror for Magistrates*, or rather that part of i
contributed by Thomas Sackville, Lord Buckhurst . . . Th
Induction and the *Complaint of Buckingham*, which Sackvill
furnished to it in 1559, though they were not published til
four years later, completely outweigh all the rest in value
His contributions to the *Mirror for Magistrates* contain the
best poetry written in the English language between Chaucer
and Spenser, and are most certainly the originals or at least
the models of some of Spenser's finest work. He has had but
faint praise of late years . . . I have little hesitation in saying
that no more astonishing contribution to English poetry,
when the due reservations of that historical criticism which is
the life of all criticism are made, is to be found anywhere.
The bulk is not great: twelve or fifteen hundred lines must
cover the whole of it. The form is not new, being merely the
7-line stanza already familiar in Chaucer. The arrangement is
in no way novel, combining as it does the allegorical presentment of embodied virtues, vices, and qualities with the
melancholy narrative common in poets for many years before.
But the poetical value of the whole is extraordinary. The two
constituents of that value, the formal and the material, are
represented here with a singular equality of development.
There is nothing here of Wyatt's floundering prosody, nothing
of the well-intentioned doggerel in which Surrey himself in-
dulges and in which his pupils simply revel. The cadences of
the verse perfect, the imagery fresh and sharp, the presentation
of nature singularly original, when it is compared with the
battered copies of the poets with whom Sackville must have
been most familiar, the followers of Chaucer from Occleeve
to Hawes. Even the general plan of the poem—the weakest
part of nearly all poems of this time—is extraordinarily effec-
tive and makes one sincerely sorry that Sackville's taste or his
other occupations did not permit him to carry out the whole
scheme on his own account. The *Induction*, in which the
author is brought face to face with Sorrow, and the central
passages of the *Complaint of Buckingham*, have a depth and
fullness of poetical sound and sense for which we must look
backwards a hundred and fifty years, or forwards nearly five
and twenty. . . .

He has not indeed the manifold music of Spenser—it would
be unreasonable to expect that he should have it. But his

tanzas are of remarkable melody, and they have about them command, a completeness of accomplishment within the writer's intentions, which is very noteworthy in so young a man. The extraordinary richness and stateliness of the measure has escaped no critic. There is indeed a certain one-sidedness about it, and a devil's advocate might urge that a long poem couched in verse (let alone the subject) of such unbroken gloom would be intolerable. But Sackville did not write a long poem, and his complete command within his limits of the effect at which he evidently aimed is most remarkable.

The second thing to note about the poem is the extraordinary freshness and truth of its imagery. From a young poet we always expect second-hand presentations of nature, and in Sackville's day second-hand presentation of nature had been elevated to the rank of a science. . . . It is perfectly clear that Thomas Sackville had, in the first place, a poetical eye to see, within as well as without, the objects of poetical presentment; in the second place, a poetical vocabulary in which to clothe the results of his seeing; and in the third place, a poetical ear by aid of which to arrange his language in the musical co-ordination necessary to poetry. Wyatt had been notoriously wanting in the last; Surrey had not been very obviously furnished with the first; and all three were not to be possessed by anyone else till Edmund Spenser arose to put Sackville's lessons in practice on a wider scale and with a less monotonous lyre. It is possible that Sackville's claims in drama may have been exaggerated—they have of late years rather been undervalued; but his claims in poetry proper can only be overlooked by those who decline to consider the most important part of poetry. In the subject of even his part of the *Mirror* there is nothing new; there is only a following of Chaucer, and Gower, and Occleeve, and Lydgate, and Hawes, and many others. But in the handling there is one novelty which makes all others of no effect or interest; it is the novelty of a new poetry.

§ iv

I often entertained wild dreams that some light might be thrown on the Shakespearean problem by a discovery of letters or documents at Knole. What more fascinating or chimerical a speculation for a literary-minded child breathing and absorbing the atmosphere of that house? I used to tell myself stories of finding Shakespeare's manuscripts up in the attics, perhaps hidden away under the flooring somewhere, or in the Muniment Room where quite rightly I was forbidden to go and rummage. Yet, as I have since discovered, my imaginings weren't so chimerical as all that. There really are some possible connections between Shakespeare and Knole. Since everything to do with Shakespeare, however slight, is of the deepest interest I offer them for what they are worth:

1. It has been suggested that Thomas Sackville was taken by Shakespeare as his model for Sir Toby Belch in "Twelfth Night"—(see the *Times Literary Supplement*, 28 March, 1929). Not a very complimentary character to attach to my respectable and so far as I know sober old ancestor; but it is quite something to figure in a Shakespeare play at all.

2. The manor of Stratford-on-Avon came into the possession of the Sackvilles in 1674, and the living of Stratford-on-Avon was presented in 1681 by Charles 6th Earl of Dorset to a certain Joseph Simcox.

3. There is a reference made by William Henry Ireland (1805) to "two letters from the pen of Shakespeare discovered some time since at Knole in Kent, among the papers of the Dorset family written by our bard to the then Lord Chamberlain (*sic*; it should be Lord Treasurer) upon mere official business relative to theatrical matters." This statement might be interesting, but as William Henry Ireland was a well-known forger of Shakespearean plays his evidence may be rejected as of negligible value.

4. Far more suggestive, I think, is *Sonnet No. CXXV* which begins:

> *Were't aught to me I bore the canopy*
> *With my extern the outward honouring.*

These lines have been taken by some commentators as a metaphor, but are they not more probably an allusion to the Conference of English and Spanish plenipotentiaries at Somerset House in 1604? (See illustration following page 128.)

is known that the King's Company of players, of which
Shakespeare was then a member, was called upon to attend
the plenipotentiaries and that Shakespeare with eleven other
fellows waited in their red liveries during the negotiations.
Now, is it not likely that a canopy was carried over the heads
of the distinguished foreigners, as was customary, and that the
duty of bearing it aloft fell to the King's players, Shakespeare
amongst them? In any case, the younger poet cannot have
failed to gaze with interest on the old statesman who in his
youth had practised the same craft of letters, and perhaps even
took the opportunity to speak to him. Whatever the answer,
we may safely say that Thomas Sackville and William
Shakespeare once in their lives came face to face.

CHAPTER IV

KNOLE IN THE REIGN OF JAMES I

RICHARD SACKVILLE, 3rd Earl *of* Dorset
and LADY ANNE CLIFFORD

§ i

IT so happens that a remarkably complete record has bee
left of existence at Knole in the early seventeenth century-
an existence compounded of extreme prodigality of livin,
tedium, and perpetual domestic quarrels. We have a priva
diary, in which every squabble and reconciliation betwee
Lord and Lady Dorset is chronicled; every gown she wor
every wager he won or lost (and he made many); every boo
she read; every game she played at Knole with the steward
with the neighbours; every time she wept; every day she "s
still, thinking the time to be very tedious." We have even
complete list of the servants and their functions, from M
Matthew Caldicott, my Lord's favourite, down to Joh
Morockoe, a Blackamoor. It would, out of this quantity o
information, be possible to reconstruct a play of singul:
accuracy.

The author of the diary was a lady of some fame and a grea
deal of character: Lady Anne Clifford, the daughter and sol
heiress of George, Earl of Cumberland, and wife to Richar
Earl of Dorset. Cumberland was himself a picturesque figur
He was Elizabeth's official champion at all jousts and tilt
ing, a nobleman of great splendour, and in addition to thi
display of truly Elizabethan glitter and parade he had th
other facet of Elizabethan *virtù*: the love of adventure, whic
carried him eleven times to sea, to the Indies and elsewher
"for the service of Queen Elizabeth," says his daughter i
the life she wrote of him, "for the good of Englan
and of his own person." She gives an account of her ow
appearance:

I was very happy in my first constitution both in mind and body, both for internal and external endowments, for never as there child more equally resembling both father and mother than myself. The colour of mine eyes were black, like my father, and the form and aspect of them was quick and lively, like my mother's; the hair of my head was brown and very thick, and so long that it reached to the calf of my legs when I stood upright, with a peak of hair on my forehead and a dimple in my chin like my father, full cheeks and round face like my mother, and an exquisite shape of body resembling my father.

After this description, more remarkable for exactness perhaps than for modesty, she adds:

But now time and age hath long since ended all these beauties, which are to be compared to the grass of the field (*Isaiah* xl., 6, 7, 8; 1 *Peter* i., 24). For now when I caused these memorables of my self to be written I have passed the 63rd year of my age.

Having put this in by way of a saving clause, she proceeds again complacently:

And though I say it, the perfections of my mind were much above those of my body; I had a strong and copious memory, a sound judgement, and a discerning spirit, and so much of a strong imagination in me as that many times even my dreams and apprehensions beforehand proved to be true; so as old Mr. John Denham, a great astronomer, that sometime lived in my father's house, would often say that I had much in me in nature to show that the sweet influences of the Pleiades and the bands of Orion were powerful both at my conception and my nativity.

She was innocent of unnecessary diffidence. Yet she was not without gratitude:

I must not forget to acknowledge that in my infancy and youth, and a great part of my life, I have escaped many dangers, both by fire and water, by passage in coaches and falls from

horses, by burning fevers, and excessive extremity of bleedin[g]
many times to the great hazard of my life, all which, and man[y]
cunning and wicked devices of my enemies, I have escape[d]
and passed through miraculously, and much the better by th[e]
help and prayers of my devout mother, who incessantl[y]
begged of God for my safety and preservation (*Jas.* v., 16).

To her mother she seems to have been excessively devoted,
and indeed, in the midst of this stubborn and peremptor[y]
character, the most vulnerable spot is her tenderness for he[r]
relations; those of her relations, that is to say, with whom sh[e]
was not at mortal enmity.

The death of Queen Elizabeth, which occurred when Ann[e]
Clifford was a girl of thirteen, was a disappointment to her i[n]
more ways than one, for "if Queen Elizabeth had lived sh[e]
intended to prefer me to be of the Privy Chamber, for at tha[t]
time there was as much hope and expectation of me as of any
other young lady whatsoever," and moreover "my Mother
and Aunt of Warwick being mourners, I was not allowed to be
one, because I was not high enough, which did much trouble
me then." She was not even allowed the privilege of watching
by the great Queen's body after it had come "by night in a
Barge from Richmond to Whitehall, my Mother and a great
Company of Ladies attending it, where it continued a great
while standing in the Drawing Chamber, where it was watched
all night by several Lords and Ladies, my Mother sitting up
with it two or three nights, but my Lady would not give me
leave to watch, by reason I was held too young." It is to be
regretted that the writer, who possessed so vivid and unself-
conscious a pen, should have been thus defrauded of setting
upon record the scene in which the old Queen, stiff as an
effigy, and blazing with the jewels of England, lay for the last
time in state, by the light of candles, among the great nobles
whom in her lifetime she had bullied and governed, and
whom even in death the rigidity of that dejezabelled presence
could still overawe.

Although she had not been allowed to see the dead Queen,
Lady Anne was taken to see the new King, but did not find
the court to her liking:

We all went to Tibbalds to see the King, who used my
Mother and Aunt very graciously, but we all saw a great
change between the fashion of the Court as it is now and of
that in the Queen's time, for we were all lousy by sitting in
the chamber of Sir Thomas Erskine.

This unpropitious introduction was the first she had to
James I, but it was by no means her last meeting with him,
for she relates several later on which might more properly be
called encounters.

About two years after Elizabeth's death Lord Cumberland
died, "very patiently and willingly of a bloody flux," leaving
Anne Clifford his only surviving child and heiress, then being
aged about fifteen years. Her father cannot have been much
more than a name to her, for although "endowed with many
perfections of nature befitting so noble a personage, as an
excellent quickness of wit and apprehension, an active and
strong body, and an affable disposition and behaviour," he
"fell to love a lady of quality," which created a breach between
himself and his wife, and "when my Mother and he did meet,
their countenance did show the dislike they had one of
another, yet he would speak to me in a slight fashion and give
me his blessing. . . . My Father used to come to us sometimes
at Clerkenwell, but not often, for he had at this time as it were
wholly left my Mother, yet the house was kept still at his
charge." All this early part of her life, I ought to explain, is
related by her in the Lives of her parents and herself, which
she compiled in her old age; and partly from a diary of
reminiscences, a transcript of which is at Knole, and which
she appears to have written at the same time as the more detailed Diary which she was then (1616–1619) keeping from
day to day. She had a happy childhood with her mother, and
cousins of her own age—"All this time we were merry at
North Hall. My Coz. Frances Bouchier and my Coz. Francis
Russell and I did use to walk much in the garden, and were
great with one another. I used to wear my Hair-coloured Velvet
every day, and learned to sing and play on the Bass-Viol of
Jack Jenkins, my Aunt's boy."

The Diary at Knole jumps without any warning or transition from the reminiscences of youth to 1616. It begins with a sad little hint of the weariness that was to follow: "All the time I stayed in the country I was sometimes merry and sometimes sad, as I had news from London." She had then been married for seven years to Richard Sackville, third Earl of Dorset, grandson to Queen Elizabeth's old Treasurer, who was himself anxious for the match, writing to Sir George Moore about "that virtuous young lady, the Lady Anne Clifford," and soliciting Moore's good offices with Lady Cumberland.

There were, in all, five children of the marriage: three little boys, who all "died young at Knole where they were born," and two little girls, of whom Margaret, born in 1614, figured largely in the Diary and is the only one to concern us, since Isabel was not born till some years after Lady Anne had ceased to keep the Diary. Lady Anne's mother travelled to London from the North in order to be present at the birth of Margaret, the first child; but by a strange mischance the journey was rendered vain, for, having gone "into the Tower of London to see some friends there, where, the gates being shut up by an accident that happened, she was kept there till after her daughter was delivered of her first child, though she had made a journey purposely from Appleby Castle, in Westmoreland, to London." Not only does the Diary contain constant references to this little girl, but Lady Anne's letters to her mother, now at Appleby, are rarely without some comment—

she begins to break out very much upon her head, which I hope will make her very healthful [a curious theory]. She hath yet no teeth come out, but they are most of them swelled in the flesh, so that now and then they make her very froward. I have found your Ladyship's words true about the nurse I had for her, for she hath been one of the most unhealthfullest women that I think ever was, and so extremely troubled with the toothache and rheums and swelling in her face as could be, and one night she fell very ill, and was taken like an ague so as she had but little milk left, and so I was enforced to send

or the next woman that was by to give my child suck, whom
hath continued with her ever since, and I thank God the child
grees so well with her milk as may be, so I mean not to
change her any more. It is a miracle to me that the child
should prosper so well. She is but a little one, I confess, but
a livelier and merrier thing was there never yet seen.

Dorset also was fond of the little girl, for in other letters to her
mother Anne says, after apologizing for her bad writing, which
she terms "scribbling," "my Lord is as fond of her as can be,
and calls her his mistress"; and again, "My Lord to her is a
very kind, loving, and dear father, and in everything will I
commend him, saving only in this business of my land,
wherein I think some evil spirit works, for in this he is as
violent as possible, so I must either do it next term or else
break friendship and love with him"; and Dorset was, on his
side, of the same opinion, for in a letter written to her at
Knole, which begins "Sweet Heart," and sends messages to
the child, he adds to his wife, "whom in all things I love and
hold a sober woman, your land only excepted, which trans-
ports you beyond yourself, and makes you devoid of all
reason." It would appear that but for this unfortunate question
of the lands and money they might have lived happily together, affection not lacking, and on Anne's part at any rate
good will not lacking either, as witness her constant defence
of him, even to her mother:

It is true that they have brought their matters so about that
I am in the greatest strait that ever poor creature was, but
whatsoever you may think of my Lord, I have found him, do
find him, and think I shall find him, the best and most worthy
man that ever breathed, therefore, if it be possible, I beseech
you, have a better opinion of him, if you know all I do, I am
sure you would believe this that I write, but I durst not impart
my mind about when I was with you, because I found you so
bitter against him, or else I could have told you so many arguments of his goodness and worth that you should have seen it
plainly yourself.

They were married when she was nineteen and he was
twenty, and two days after their marriage he succeeded to his

father's titles and estates: "We have no other news here but of weddings and burials, the Earl of Dorset died on Monday night leaving a heaire [?] widow God wot, and his son seeing him past hope the Saturday before married the Lady Anne Clifford." In spite, however, of all they had to make life pleasant—their youth, their wealth, and the privileges of their position—they spent the succeeding years in making it as unpleasant as they possibly could for one another.

I hardly think that it is necessary or even interesting to go into the legal details of the long dispute over Lord Cumberland's will. The interest of Anne and Richard Dorset is human, not litigious. It may therefore be sufficient to say that by the terms of his will Lord Cumberland bequeathed the vast Clifford estates in Westmoreland to his brother Sir Francis Clifford, with the proviso that they should revert to Anne, his daughter, in the event of the failure of heirs male, a reversion which eventually took place, thirty-eight years after his death. What he does not appear to have realized was that the estates were already entailed upon Lady Anne; and that he was, by his will, illegally breaking an entail which dated back to the reign of Edward II.

It is easy to judge, from this broad indication, the infinite possibilities for litigation amongst persons contentiously minded. Such persons were not lacking. There was Lady Cumberland, Anne's mother, bent upon safeguarding the rights of her daughter. There was Francis, the new Earl of Cumberland, equally bent upon preserving what had been left to him by will. There was Richard Dorset, whose own fortune was not adequate to his extravagance, and who, having married an heiress, was determined for his own sake that that heiress should not be defrauded of her inheritance, or that, if she was to be defrauded, he at least should receive ample compensation. And finally there was Anne herself, who was more resolved than any of them that she and the North of England should not be parted. Dorset's part, of the four, was the most elaborate, and the most discreditable. He would have been willing for his wife to renounce some of her claims return for the compromise of ready cash. Anne, however, remained single-hearted throughout: she was the legal heiress of the North, and the North she would have; and in the midst of the otherwise sordid and mercenary dispute, in which Dorset used every means of coercion, she remains fixed in her perfectly definite attitude of obstinacy, unswayed by her husband, his relations, her own relations, their friends, the Archbishop of Canterbury, and the King himself, their remonstrances, their threats, their vindictiveness, and the actual injuries she had to endure over a long stretch of years. In the end she got the better of them all, and the last picture of her left by the "Lives" is that of a triumphant and imperious old lady, retired to the stronghold of her northern castles, where her authority could stand "against sectaries, almost against parliaments and armies themselves"; refusing to go to court unless she might wear blinkers"; moving with feudal, with almost royal, state between her many castles, from Appleby to Pendragon, from Pendragon to Brougham, from Brougham to Brough, from Brough to Skipton; building brew-houses, wash-houses, bake-houses, kitchens, stables; sending word to Cromwell that as fast as he should knock her castles about her ears she would surely put them up again; endowing almshouses; ruling over her almswomen and her tenants; receiving, like the patriarchal old despot that she was, the generations of her children, her grandchildren, and her great-grandchildren.

Before she could reach these serene waters, however, she had many storms to weather, and to bear the "crosses and contradictions" which caused her to write "the marble pillars of Knole in Kent and Wilton in Wiltshire were to me oftentimes but the gay arbours of anguish." Richard Sackville in his own day was a byword for extravagance, and was bent on extorting from his wife for the purposes of his pleasure the utmost resources of her inheritance. His portrait is at Knole, a full-length by Van Somer; he has a pale, pointed face, dark hair growing in a peak, and small mean eyes, and is dressed entirely in black with enormous silver rosettes on his shoes. There is also the very beautiful miniature of him by Isaac

Oliver in the Victoria and Albert Museum, showing the rich
ness of his clothes, his embroidered stockings, and his hand
resting upon the extravagantly-plumed helmet on the table
beside him.

His life is an empty record of gambling, cock-fighting
tilting; of balls and masques, women and fine clothes. "Above
all they speak of the Earl of Dorset," says a contemporary
letter, after describing the lavishness of some of the costumes
worn in a Court masque in which he was taking part, "but
their extreme cost and riches make us all poor," and Clarendon
says of him, "his excess of expenditure, in all the ways to
which money could be applied, was such that he so entirely
consumed almost the whole great fortune which descended
to him, that when he was forced to leave the title to his
younger brother he left, in a manner, nothing to him to sup
port it." The enormous estates which he inherited, the careful
accumulation of the old Lord Treasurer, he sold in great part
in order to squander the proceeds upon his amusements
before he had been in possession for three years he had sold
the manor of Sevenoaks, and had "conveyed" Knole itself to
one Henry Smith (retaining, however, the house at a rent of
£100 a year for his own use), and in the course of rather less
than ten years he had sold estates, including much of Fleet
Street and the Manor of Holborn, to the value of £80,616
or nearly a million of modern money.

In Aubrey's *Bodleian Letters* there is an anecdote concerning
him, not devoid of humour:

He [Sir Kenelm Digby] married that celebrated beauty
and courtesan, Mrs. Venetia Stanley, whom Richard, Earl of
Dorset, kept as his concubine, had children by her, and settled
on her an annuity of £500 per annum; which after Sir Kenelm
Digby married her was unpaid by the Earl: Sir Kenelm Digby
sued the Earl, after marriage, and recovered it. Venetia Stanley
was a most beautiful and desirable creature . . . sanguine and
tractable, and of much suavity.

In those days Richard, Earl of Dorset, lived in the greatest
splendour of any nobleman of England.

After her marriage she [Venetia Stanley] redeemed her

onour by her strict living. Once a year the Earl of Dorset
invited her and Sir Kenelm to dinner, where the Earl would
behold her with much passion, yet only kiss her hand.

Later on in his life a certain Lady Peneystone appears,
who considerably complicated the already difficult relations
between Anne and himself.

Anne Clifford herself, in spite of all that she had to endure
at his hands, gives a charitable account of him.

This first lord of mine was in his own nature of a just mind,
of a sweet disposition, and very valiant in his own person.

He was . . . so great a lover of scholars and soldiers, as that
with an excessive bounty towards them, or indeed any of
worth that were in distress, he did much to diminish his estate,
as also with excessive prodigality in housekeeping, and other
noble ways at court, as tilting, masqueing, and the like, Prince
Henry being then alive, who was much addicted to these
exercises, and of whom he was much beloved.

What his wife says of his being a great lover of scholars is
borne out by his friendship with and patronage of Beaumont,
Ben Jonson, Fletcher, and Drayton. Donne was an intimate
friend, and is stated by Isaac Walton to have left Lord Dorset
several pictures in his will. Nothing else remains to Richard's
credit. Henry King's epitaph on his most honoured friend
Richard, Earl of Dorset is fulsome rather than truthful, though it
was generous of King not to mention that he had lent Dorset
£1000 which apparently was never repaid. He is utterly
eclipsed—weak, vain, and prodigal—by the interest of that
woman of character, his wife, knowing so well to "discourse
of all things, from predestination to slea[1] silk," and by the
faithful picture that is her Diary.

§ ii

She is living (1616) principally at Knole, sometimes in
London, sometimes making an expedition into the North to

[1] Slea = unravelled.

join her mother, who in all her difficulties was her counsello[r]
and ally. The perpetual topic of the diary is the dispute wit[h]
her husband:

"My Coz: Russell came to me the same day, and chid me
and told me of all my faults and errors, he made me wee[p]
bitterly, then I spoke a prayer of Owens, and came home b[y]
water where I took an extreme Cold."

The Archbishop [of Canterbury] my Lord William Howard[,]
my Lord Rous, my Coz: Russell, my brother Sackville, and [a]
great company of men were all in the gallery at Dorset House[,]
where the Archbishop took me aside and talked with m[e]
privately one hour and half, and persuaded me both by Divine
and human means to set my hand to their arguments. But m[y]
answer to his Lordship was that I would do nothing unti[l]
my Lady [her mother] and I had conferred together. Much
persuasion was used by him and all the company, sometimes
terrifying me and sometimes flattering me.

Next day was a marvellous day to me, for it was generally
thought that I must either have sealed the argument or else
have parted from my Lord.

She then starts for the North—a hazardous journey—to
confer with her mother.

We had two coaches in our company with four horses apiece
and about twenty-six horsemen. I came to my lodgings [at
Derby] with a heavy heart considering how many things stood
between my Lord and I.

We went from the Parsons' House near the Dangerous
Moors, being eight miles and afterwards the ways so dangerous
the horses were fain to be taken out of the coach to be lifted
down the hills. This day Rivers' horse fell from a bridge into
river. We came to Manchester about ten at night.

Dorset was not above subjecting her to petty annoyances
and humiliations, for he sends messengers after her with
"letters to show it was my Lord's pleasure that the men and
horses should come away without me, so after much falling
out betwixt my Lady [her mother] and them, all the folks went
away, there being a paper drawn to show that they went away

y my Lord's direction and contrary to my will.[1] At night I
ent two messengers to my folks to entreat them to stay. For
ome two nights my mother and I lay together, and had much
alk about this business."

In order to get back to London she has to borrow a coach
rom her mother, from whom she takes a "grievous and heavy
arting." Arrived at Knole, "I had a cold welcome from my
ord," and a day or two later he takes his departure for Lon-
on, sending constant messengers and letters, to know whether
he will give way to his demands. "About this time," she sadly
rites—it is April, spring at Knole, and she then aged twenty-
ix—"about this time I used to rise early in the morning and
o to the Standing in the garden, and taking my prayer book
ith me beseech God to be merciful to me and to help me as
He always hath done."

Meanwhile Dorset's threats increase in virulence: on the
irst of May he sends Mr. Rivers to tell her she shall live
either at Knole nor at Bolbrook; on the second he sends Mr.
egg to tell the servants he will come down once more to see
er, which shall be the last time; and on the third he sends
Peter Basket, his gentleman of the horse, with a letter to say
it was his pleasure that the Child should go the next day to
ondon . . . when I considered that it would both make my
ord more angry with me and be worse for the Child I re-
olved to let her go; after I had sent for Mr. Legg and talked
ith him about that and other matters I wept bitterly."

On the fourth ". . . the Child went into the litter to go to
ondon." There is no comment. It must have been a pathetic
ittle departure.

---

[1] The original of this curious paper is now at Appleby, dated April
st, 1616, and runs as follows: "A memoranda that I, Anne, Countess
f Dorset, sole daughter and heir to George, late Earl of Cumberland,
o take witness of all these gentlemen present, that I both desire and
ffer myself to go up to London with my men and horses, but they,
aving received a contrary commandment from my Lord, my husband,
ill by no means consent nor permit me to go with them. Now my
esire is that all the world may know that this stay of mine proceeds
nly from my husband's command, contrary to my consent or
greement, whereof I have gotten these names underwritten to testify
he same."

On the ninth she received, besides the news that her mother was dangerously ill, "a letter from my Lord to let me know his determination was the Child should go to live at Horsley and not come hither any more, so as this was a very grievous and sorrowful day to me." An unusual bitterness escapes from her pen:

All this time my Lord was in London where he had all and infinite great resort coming to him. He went much abroad to Cocking and Bowling Alleys, to plays and horse races, and commended by all the world. I stayed in the country, having many times a sorrowful and heavy heart, and being condemned by most folks because I would not consent to the agreement, so as I may truly say I am like an owl in the desert.

And a few days later:

My Lord came down from London, my Lord lying in Leslie Chamber and I in my own. My Lord and I after supper had some talk, we fell out and parted for that night.

There was worse to come, for at the end of the month her mother died, "which I held as the greatest and most lamentable cross that could have befallen me," and, mixed up with this sorrow, which is evidently genuine, is the fear that she may be definitely dispossessed of the inheritance of her forefathers. She found, however, that she had the disposal of the body, "which was some contentment to my aggrieved soul." Her sorrows begin to lighten. Dorset, probably perceiving his bullying to be worse than useless against a woman of her mettle, tries a different tack: "My Lord assured me how kind and good a husband he would be to me"; they patch up a reconciliation, and she makes over to him certain of her Cumberland estates in default of heirs; they agree that Mrs. Bathurst, apparently a bone of contention, should "go away from the Child . . . so that my Lord and I were never greater friends than at this time . . . and my Lord brought me down to the coach side where we had a loving and kind parting." He even joined her in the North, and she records how at Appleby Castle she set up the "green velvet bed where the

me night we went to lie there," and how "in the afternoon I
rought stitchwork and my Lord sat and read by me."

She gives many particulars of how she spent her days in
e North. I fancy she was a good deal happier there, and
ore at home, and consequently more light-hearted, than at
nole. At the same time she was anxious to go back to London
rejoin Dorset, but this for some reason he was not disposed
allow. She consoled herself with innocuous occupations:

This month I spent in working and reading. Mr. Dunbell
ad a great part of the *History of the Netherlands*. . . . Upon
e 1st I rose by times in the morning and went up to the
agan Tower to my prayers, and saw the sun rise. . . . Upon
e 4th I sat in the Drawing Chamber all the day at my work.
. . Upon the 9th I sat at my work and heard Rivers and
Marsh read Montaigne's *Essays*, which book they have read
most this fortnight. . . . Upon the 12th I made an end of my
ashion of Irish stitch, it being my chief help to pass away the
me at work. . . . Upon the 21st was the first day I put on my
lack silk grogram gown. . . . Upon the 20th I spent most of
e day in playing at Tables. All this time since my Lord went
way I wore my black Taffety night-gown[1] and a yellow
affety waistcoat and used to rise betimes in the morning and
alk upon the leads and afterwards to hear reading. Upon the
3rd I did string the pearls and diamonds left me by my
other into a necklace.

t last the summons came, and "upon the 24th Basket set out
om London to Brougham Castle to fetch me up. I bought of
Ir. Cleborn who came to see me a clock and a save-Guard
=cloak] of cloth laced with black lace to keep me warm on
y journey." Dorset sent in the retinue to fetch her, moreover,
cook, a baker, and a Tom Fool.

Her arrival in London was auspicious: Dorset and a com-
any of relatives came out to meet her at Islington, so that
here were in all ten or eleven coaches, and when she arrived
t Dorset House she found the house "well dressed up against
came," and the Child met her in the gallery. Moreover, "all

[1] Night-gown, of course, has not the modern meaning, as at that
ate people slept naked.

this time of my being at London I was much sent to and visite
by many" (the young heiress, whose matrimonial disputes ha
raised so much dust at Court, was an object of interest an
curiosity), and she made friends: "My Lady Manners cam
in the morning to dress my head. I had a new black wroug
Taffety gown which my Lady St. John's tailor made. She us
often to come to me, and I to her, and was very kind one
another." Such troubles as she had were but slight: "I din
above in my chamber and wore my night-gown because I w
not very well, which day and yesterday I forgot that it w
fish day and ate flesh at both dinners. In the afternoon I play
at Glecko[1] with my Lady Gray and lost £27 odd money." S
far, so good. She gave a sweet-bag to the Queen for a Ne
Year's gift, and was kissed by the King. She went to see th
play of the Mad Lover; she went to the Tower to see Lor
and Lady Somerset, lying there since their arraignment; sh
went to the Court to see Lord Villiers created Earl of Buckin
ham; she ate a "scrambling supper" and went to see th
Masque on Twelfth Night. She betrays with an unsophi
ticated and rather charming ingenuity her delight in the
things. But the storm scowled at her over the rim of the hor
zon, and presently it broke. The first entries are like th
splash of the first big rain-drops: "We came from London
Knole; this night my Lord and I had a falling out about th
land." Next day she has Mr. Sandy's book about the goverr
ment of the Turks read aloud to her, but "my Lord sat th
most part of the day reading in his closet." Next day his sull
materialized, and he "went up to London upon the sudde
we not knowing it till the afternoon."

Six days later—there are no entries in the diary to recor
the suspense of these six days—she is sent for to London
see the King, a higher test for her strength of mind, even, tha
the former persuasions of the Archbishop of Canterbury. Wi
she capitulate at last? or will she come out with her flag sti
flying? the tongues of London wagged. The interview is be
given in her own words:

[1] *Glecko*, or *Gleck*: a three-handed game played with 44 car
(eight left in stock). The gleck consisted in three of a kind.

Upon the 17th when I came up, my Lord told me I must solve to go to the King next day. Upon the 18th being turday, I went presently after dinner to the Queen to the rawing Chamber where my Lady Derby told the Queen how y business stood, and that I was to go to the King, so she omised me she would do all the good in it she could. When had stayed but a little while there I was sent for out, my ord and I going through my Lord Buckingham's chamber, ho brought us into the King, being in the Drawing Chamber. e put out all those that were there, and my Lord and I neeled by his chair side, when he persuaded us both to peace nd to put the whole matter wholly into his hands, which my ord consented to, but I beseeched His Majesty to pardon e *for that I would never part from Westmoreland while I lived pon any condition whatsoever*, sometimes he used fair means nd persuasions and sometimes foul means, but I was resolved efore, so, as nothing would move me, from the King we vent to the Queen's side, and brought my Lady St. John o her lodging and so we went home.

There is a little note at the side of this entry: "The Queen ave me warning not to trust matters absolutely to the King est he should deceive me."

The affair was not allowed to rest there. Two days later she vas again summoned before the King, and a sour, unedifying pectacle the majesty of James I must have presented, thus onfronted with the young obstinacy of the heiress of Westmoreland:

I was sent for up to the King into his Drawing Chamber, where the door was locked and nobody suffered to stay here out my Lord and I, my Uncle Cumberland, my Coz: Clifford, my Lords Arundel, Pembroke and Montgomery, Sir John Digby. For lawyers there were my Lord Chief Justice Montague, and Hobart Yelverton the King's Solicitor, Sir Randal Crewe that was to speak for my Lord and I. The King asked us all if we would submit to his judgement in this case, my uncle Cumberland, my Coz: Clifford, and my Lord answered they would, but I would never agree to it without Westmoreland, at which the King grew in a great chaff. My Lord of Pembroke and the King's solicitor speaking much against me, at last when they saw there was no remedy, my Lord, fearing

the King would do me some public disgrace, desired Sir Jo[
Digby would open the door, who went out with me and p[
suaded me much to yield to the King. Presently after my Lo[
came from the King, when it was resolved that if I would n[
come to an agreement there should be an agreement ma[
without me.

After these encounters she retired to Knole, while Dors[
remained in London, "being in extraordinary grace and favo[
with the King." She, poor thing, resumed at Knole the pitif[
monotony of her country existence, which to a mind [
vigorous must have been irksome in the extreme, and t[
Diary becomes again the record of her small occupatio[
threaded with the worry and sorrow of her dissensions wi[
her husband. It is illuminating that she never criticizes hin[
there are references to his "worth and nobleness of di[
position"; her spirit, although high and emancipated enoug[
to stand out against the King in the defence of Westmorelan[
could not conceive revolt against the subjection of matrimon[
It is an idea which never once enters her head. She eve[
writes him a letter to give him "humble thanks for his nob[
usage toward me in London"; but a very little while after th[
"Thomas Woodgate came from London and brought a squir[
rel to the Child, and my Lord wrote me a letter by which [
perceived my Lord was clean out with me, and how much m[
enemies have wrought against me."

Conscientious as she is, she no longer finds enough event[
to justify a daily entry. Perhaps—who knows? for my part[
strongly suspect it—her fighing spirit preferred even the[
ordeals and excitements of London to the tedium of Knole[
She has very little to tell: only the gowns she wore, the book[
she read, the games she played with the steward, and the[
ailments of the Child.

At this time I wore a plain green flannel gown that William[
Pinn made me and my yellow taffety waistcoat. Rivers used[
to read to me in Montaigne's *Essays*, and Moll Neville in the[
Fairy Queen. The Child had a bitter fit of her ague again[
insomuch I was fearful of her that I could hardly sleep all night[
and I beseeched God Almighty to be merciful and spare her life[

is ague of the Child's is a constant preoccupation. I suppose
that it was a kind of convulsion, for which the cure was a "salt
powder to put in her beer." On certain days a return of it
appears to have been confidently expected, for I find: "upon
the 4th should have been the Child's fit, but she missed it,"
and two days later she has "a grudging of her ague." There is
a good deal about the Child—never referred to under any
other designation until she attains her 5th birthday, after
which she is promoted to "my Lady Margaret." The portrait
of her which is here reproduced hangs over the fireplace in
Lady Betty Germaine's sitting-room; her ring dangles on a
ribbon round her neck, and her hair is done in an elaborate
manner which defied all my efforts, when I was the same age,
to do my own in the same way.

She was an amusement and a consolation, as well as a source
of anxiety, to her mother. Her garments are carefully noted:

The 28th was the first time the Child put on a pair of whale-
bone bodice. . . . The Child put on her red bays coat. . . . I
cut the Child's strings from off her coats and made her use
togs alone, so as she had two or three falls at first but had no
hurt with them. . . . The Child put on her first coats that were
laced, with lace being of red bays. . . . I began to dress my
head with a roll without a wire. I wrote not to my Lord because
he wrote not to me since he went away. After supper I went
out with the child who rode a pie-bald nag. The 14th, the
Child came to lie with me which was the first time that ever
she lay all night in a bed with me since she was born;

and another time she speaks of "the time being very tedious
with me, as having neither comfort nor company, only the
Child."

For the rest, she was thrown back upon her own resources.
Dorset came and went, and in between whiles there are small,
vivid pictures of existence at Knole:

After supper I walked in the garden and gathered cherries,
and talked with Josiah [the French page] who told me he
thought all the men in the house loved me.

And again:

About this time [April 1617] my Lord made the steward alter most of the rooms in the house and dress them up as fine as he could and determined to make all his old clothes in purple stuff for the Gallery and Drawing Chamber.

March 1617. 5*th*. Couch puppied in the morning.

8*th*. I made an end of reading *Exodus*. After supper I played at Glecko with the steward as I often do after dinner and supper.

9*th*. I went abroad in the garden and said my prayers in the standing.

10*th*. I was not well at night, so I ate a posset and went to bed.

11*th*. The time grew tedious, so as I used to go to bed about 8 o'clock I did lie a-bed till 8 the next morning.

14*th*. I made an end of my Irish stitch cushion.

15*th*. My Lord came down to Buckhurst. This day I put on my mourning grogram gown and intend to wear it till my mourning time is out, because I was found fault with for wearing such ill clothes.

22*nd*. I began a new Irish stitch cushion.

24*th*. We made Rosemary cakes.

Two days later Dorset arrived from Buckhurst, and they walked together in the park and the garden. "I wrought much within doors and strived to sit as merry a face as I could upon a discontented heart"; but in spite of this entry they seem to have remained on fairly friendly terms until Easter.

30*th*. I spent in walking and sitting in the park, having my mind more contented than it was before my Lord came from Buckhurst.

5*th April*. My Lord went up to my closet and said how little money I had left contrary to all they had told him, sometimes I had fair words from him and sometimes foul, but I took all patiently, and did strive to give him as much content and assurance of my love as I could possibly, yet *I told him I would never part with Westmoreland*. After supper, because my Lord was sullen and not willing to go into the nursery, I had Mary bring the Child to him in my chamber.

7*th*. My Lord lay in my chamber.

13*th*. My Lord supped privately with me in the Drawing
Chamber, and had much discourse of the manners of the
folks at court.

By the 17*th*, My Lord told me he was resolved never to move
me more in these business because he saw how fully I was bent,

But evidently he did not stick to this good resolution, because;
April 20th, Easter-day, "My Lord and I had a great falling-
out," and a few days later, "This night my Lord should have
lain with me, but he and I fell out about matters."

By the next day, however, they were friends again; they
played at Burley Break upon the lawn; and "this night my
Lord came in to lie in my chamber." The next day, too, was
spent in peace, and she "spent the evening in working and
going down to my Lord's closet, where I sat and read much
of the Turkish history, and Chaucer."

So it goes on. It becomes, perhaps, a little monotonous,
save that it is always so human, and so modern. One sym-
pathizes with her in her weaknesses even more than in her
defiance; when, for instance, she writes amicable letters to all
her relations-in-law, sending them locks of the Child's hair,
being "desirous to win the love of my Lord's kindred by all
the fair means I could," in reality stealing a march upon
Dorset in order to get them on her side. One day she chronicles,
"This night I went into a bath," but whether this event was of
such rarity as to deserve special mention is not explained. At
Whitsuntide they all went to church, but "my eyes were so
blubbered with weeping that I could scarce look up," and in
the afternoon of the same day they again "fell out." But she
consoles herself with new clothes—or was that an additional
penance? for she was never given to personal vanity—"I
essayed on my sea-water green satin gown and my damask
embroidered with gold, both which gowns the tailor which
was sent from London made fit for me to wear with open
cuffs after the French fashion." Little peace-offerings came
from time to time from Dorset; on one occasion he sends
half a buck, with an indifferent kind letter," and on another
occasion "My Lord sent Adam to trim the Child's hair, and
sent me the dewselts of two deer and wrote me a letter between

kindness and unkindness." "Still working and being e
tremely melancholy" is the entry of one summer day, and
day later, "Still working and sad." A little after this she "ro
on horseback to Withyham to see my Lord Treasurer's tom
and went down into the vault, and came home again [
Knole] weeping the most part of the day." This is perhaps n
very surprising. I have been down into that vault myself, an
it is not a cheerful expedition. In a small, dark cave unde
ground, beneath the church, among grey veils of cobweb
the coffins of the Sackvilles are stacked on shelves; they g
back to the fourteenth century, and are of all sizes, from full
grown men down to the tiny ones lapped in lead. But, c
course, when Anne Clifford went there there were not so man
as there are now; the pompous ones were not yet in their places
with their rusty coronets, save those of the old Treasurer an
his son; and their blood did not run in the veins of Lady Anne
so on the whole she had less reason to be impressed than I

The Diary continues in very much the same strain until i
comes to an end with December 1619, the year 1618 being
entirely missed out. By that time both Dorset and Anne were
in bad health; but whereas he was to die five years later, at the
age of thirty-five, she, made of tougher stuff, was to survive
him by fifty-two years. His last letter to her, written to her on
the very day of his death, shows all the affection which was so
undermined by that question of her lands:

Sweet Heart,   26th March, 1624

I thank you for your letter. I had resolved to come down to
Knole, and to have received the Blessed Sacrament, but God
hath prevented it with sickness, for on Wednesday night I fell
into a fit of casting, which held me long, then last night I had
a fit of fever. I have for my physician Dr. Baskerville and Dr.
Fox. I thank God I am now at good ease, having rested well
this morning. I would not have you trouble yourself till I have
occasion to send for you. You shall in the meantime hear daily
from me. So, with my love to you, and God's blessing and mine
to both my children, I commend you to God's protection.

Your assured loving husband

RICHARD DORSET.

"His debts," says one Chamberlain, writing to Sir Dudley Carleton, "are £60,000, so that he does not leave much." In his will he bequeaths to his "dearly beloved wife all her wearing apparel and such rings and jewels as were hers on her marriage, and the rock ruby ring which I have given her," also "my carriage made by Mefflyn, lined with green cloth and laced with green and black silk lace, and my six bay coach geldings."

§ iii

Her portraits change as her years advance, and the lines of determination harden about her mouth. Her true life—the life for which she was most truly fitted—only began after she had passed her fiftieth year, when with the death of her kinsman Lord Cumberland the northern estates passed calmly and naturally into her hands at last. All the quarrels and litigation and anxiety of her youth were left behind her; she had buried Lord Dorset; she had buried Lord Pembroke after a second marriage as disastrous and as contentious as the first; she had borne Sackville children and Herbert children; she had been long-suffering though adamant, submissive, though immovable; she had moped in the sumptuous prisons that were Knole and Wilton; now she was free to turn tyrant herself over her own undisputed realm. She wasted nothing of the opportunity. Away from London, away from the influence of the Court, entrenched in her numerous castles in the North, she ruled autocratically over her servants, her tenants, her neighbours, and the generations and ramifications of her family. No detail of comings and goings, no penny of expenditure escaped her vigilant eye or her recording pen; and her diary, that document of intimacy, autocracy, piety, and exactitude, carries its entries down to the very day before her death. With public or political events she scarcely ever concerned herself, but on the other hand no detail of her own private life or of the existence of those around her was too small to excite her comment. Whether her laundry-maids went to church, whether she pared her finger and toe nails, whether her dog puppied, whether she received letters, whether she washed her feet and legs (this is on the 22nd of February, the last occasion being on the 13th of December preceding), whether she kissed the sempstress—all is noted with the same precision and gravity. No anniversary or coincidence is allowed to pass unobserved. That amazing memory extended back over three score years; and, moreover, she had the immense volumes of her notebooks for reference, date for date. Her past was ever present to her, the agreeable and the disagreeable merged into one landscape of consonant tone, and whether she observed that this day sixty years ago she travelled with her blessed mother, or fell out with Dorset, it is with the same complacency and satisfaction at having the tiny anniversary to record. This vigorous mind was not, perhaps, planned on a very broad scale. It was self-centred and self-sufficient; severe but not reckless; no fine carelessness endears her to us, or surprises; even her acts of generosity, and they were numerous, are recorded with the same scrupulous accuracy. She could not give two shillings to a child without setting it down. Her generosity, like all her other acts, was methodical: she rewarded her servants for definite services with extra wages; she kept ready to hand a supply of little presents, because it was contrary to her ideas of hospitality that any visitor, however humble, should go away empty-handed, and was careful to consider what particular gift would be most acceptable to the recipient, frequently choosing something of practical utility, such as gloves or lengths of cloth for women, money or ruffles for men; and these idiosyncrasies run true all through her character, for, conversely, although she was prepared to be generous in her treatment of others she was equally determined that she herself should be fairly treated by them, and frequent are the entries in her diary to this effect: "In the morning did I see Mr. Robert Willison of Penrith paid for a rundlet of sack, but I was very angry with him because I thought it too dear, and told him I would have no more of him, and then he slipped away from me in a good hurry." She would always pay cash too, and bullied her special almswomen, whom she

ould not allow to ask for credit with the tradesmen of
ppleby.

Her rights were her rights, and she had always had a great
dea of them. One recognizes the spirit that told the King she
would never be parted from Westmoreland," in the old litigant
hat went unhesitatingly and repeatedly to law over niceties
onnected with small portions of her estates, content to spend
arge sums of money in lawyers' fees if only she could succeed
—as she invariably did—in proving her point. There is one
tory which illustrates both her tenacity and her humour—
he story of a certain tenant whose rent included a hen due
early to the lady of the manor. This tribute he neglected to
and over. Lady Anne instantly had the law on him, spent
400 in enforcing her claim, won her case, received the hen,
nvited her defeated opponent to dinner with her, and caused
he bird to be cooked for them both as the staple dish of the
heal.

So the tranquil and crowded years spun themselves out for
er, and she grew to be an old woman and a contented one,
or she had attained at last the existence and occupations best
uited to her. Her life was full: the things which filled it were
mall things, perhaps, but if they satisfied her who should
avil? Her journeyings alone occupied much of her time: those
xtraordinary progresses from castle to castle, she herself
ravelling in her horse-litter, her ladies in the coach-and-six,
er menservants on horseback, her women in other coaches,
nd a rabble of small fry following, so that the miniature army
hich accompanied her amounted sometimes to as many as
hree hundred. Often this retinue would include members of
er family, or some of her neighbours; they travelled over the
noors of the North, by rough roads, "uncouth and untrodden,
hose mountainous and almost impassable ways," stopping on
he way in those highland villages which had not yet been
onoured by a visit from the great old lady or received her
ounty, and, coming at the end of the journey to Brougham,
o Brough, to Barden, to Skipton, to Pendragon, or to Appleby,
Lady Anne would receive her dependants one by one in her
wn chamber, give her hand to the men, kiss the women, and

dismiss them again to their own homes. Her health was r
longer very good, but that was never allowed to deter he
from her plans: her courage and vigour triumphed alway
over the treacherous flesh, greatly to the concern of thos
about her. On one occasion, travelling from Appleby
Brougham, she was delayed at the start by a "swounding fit,
when she had to be carried to a bed and laid there near
"great fire"; much persuasion was used that she "would n
travel on so sharp and cold a day, but she, having before fixe
on that day, and so much company being come purposely
wait on her, she would go." As she reached her litter, howeve
she fainted again, "Yet as soon as that fit was over she went.
Arrived at Brougham she fainted for the third time, but o
being upbraided by her friends and servants for her stubbor
ness in making the journey, she replied that she knew sh
must die, and it was the same thing to her to die on the wa
as in her house, in her litter or in her bed, and furthermor
would not acknowledge any necessity why she should liv
but saw every necessity for keeping to her resolution. "If sh
will, she will, you may depend on't," they said of her, "if sh
won't, she won't, and there's an end on't."

Now that there was no one to reproach her, as Dorset ha
been accustomed to reproach her, for her lack of finery an
absence of proper vanity, she dressed always in rough blac
serge, she shaved her head, her fare was of the plainest, and he
personal economy was pushed to the length of such sma
eccentricities as using up every stray scrap of paper for he
correspondence. One luxury, indeed, she permitted herself
she smoked a pipe. Into all the details of her household sh
looked with a careful eye; already in the days when she wa
living at Knole she had used up Richard Dorset's old shirt
to make clouts, now at Appleby she saw to the preserving c
fruit, she had her cheeses made at Brougham, sixteen at
time, she got her coal from her own pits, she had all delin
quents into her own room and scolded them till they wer
probably thankful to be dismissed. At the same time she neve
forgot those that had served her faithfully; she would sen
her own coach to bring some old retainer to visit her; th

arriages, morals, and vicissitudes of her meanest servant
ere a matter of interest to her; their marriage portions she
ade her own affair. Besides her servants, her own family gave
er much food for thought and preoccupation: it is true that
f her seven children only two—her two Sackville daughters—
ad lived to grow up, but they by now had produced a cohort
f grandchildren, whose visits to Lady Anne were a source of
finite pleasure to the old lady. It is, altogether, a pleasant
nd seemly end to such a life. She had attained the great age of
ighty-six; her diary was filled with religious references; she
ever dwelt upon her death, but it is clear that she can never
or one moment have dreaded it. She had lived up consistently
o her principles and to her motto: "Preserve your loyalty,
efend your rights," and was ready to go whenever the call
ould come. "I went not out all this day," is the last entry in
er diary, and the next day (22nd of March 1676), there is an
ntry in another hand, "The 22nd day the Countess died."

Her personality is still very much alive in Westmoreland.
s recently as 1956 it was suggested that electric light might
e put into the almshouses at Appleby. This offer was turned
own, "We do no think Lady Anne would have liked it."

Epitaph by Thomas Gray, on visiting her tomb on Septem-
er 3rd, 1767:

> *Now clean, now hideous, mellow now, now gruff,*
> *She swept, she Hiss'd, she ripen'd, and grew rough*
> *At Brougham, Pendragon, Appleby, and Brough.*

A Catalogue

f the Household and Family of the Right Honourable RICHARD,
ARL of DORSET, *in the year of our Lord* 1613; *and so continued
ntil the year* 1624, *at Knole, in Kent.*

At MY LORD'S TABLE

My Lord	My Lady
My Lady Margaret	My Lady Isabella
Mr. Sackville	Mr. Frost
John Musgrave	Thomas Garret

At THE PARLOUR TABLE

Mrs. Field	Mrs. Willoughby
Mrs. Grimsditch	Mrs. Stewkly
Mrs. Fletcher	Mrs. Wood

[1] Mr. Dupper, *Chaplain*
Mr. Matthew Caldicott, *my Lord's favourite*
Mr. Edward Legge, *Steward*
Mr. Peter Basket, *Gentleman of the Horse*
Mr. Marsh, *Attendant on my Lady*
Mr. Wooldridge
Mr. Cheyney
Mr. Duck, *Page*
Mr. Josiah Cooper, *a Frenchman, Page*
Mr. John Belgrave, *Page*
Mr. Billingsley
Mr. Graverner, *Gentleman Usher*
Mr. Marshall, *Auditor*
Mr. Edwards, *Secretary*
Mr. Drake, *Attendant*

At THE CLERKS' TABLE IN THE HALL

Edward Fulks and John Edwards, *Clerks of the Kitchen*
Edward Care, *Master Cook*
William Smith, *Yeoman of the Buttery*
Henry Keble, *Yeoman of the Pantry*
John Mitchell, *Pastryman*
Thomas Vinson, *Cook*
John Elnor, *Cook*
Ralph Hussie, *Cook*
John Avery, *Usher of the Hall*
Robert Elnor, *Slaughterman*
Benjamin Staples, *Groom of the Great Chamber*
Thomas Petley, *Brewer*
William Turner, *Baker*
Francis Steeling, *Gardener*
Richard Wicking, *Gardener*
Thomas Clements, *Under Brewer*
Samuel Vans, *Caterer*

[1] Could this be Brian Dupper, a poet, who became Bishop of Salisbury in 1641?

Edward Small, *Groom of the Wardrobe*
Samuel Southern, *Under Baker*
Lowry, *a French boy*

THE NURSERY

Nurse Carpenter   Widow Ben
Jane Sisley   Dorothy Pickenden

At THE LONG TABLE IN THE HALL

Robert Care, *Attendant on my Lord*
Mr. Gray, *Attendant likewise*
Mr. Roger Cook, *Attendant on my Lady Margaret*
Mr. Adam Bradford, *Barber*
Mr. John Guy, *Groom of my Lord's Bedchamber*
Walter Comestone, *Attendant on my Lady*
Edward Lane, *Scrivener*
Mr. Thomas Poor, *Yeoman of the Wardrobe*
Mr. Thomas Leonard, *Master Huntsman*
Mr. Woodgate, *Yeoman of the Great Chamber*
John Hall, *Falconer*
James Flennel, *Yeoman of the Granary*
Rawlinson, *Armourer*
Moses Shonk, *Coachman*
Anthony Ashly, *Groom of the Great Horse*
Griffin Edwards, *Groom of my Lady's Horse*
Francis Turner, *Groom of the Great Horse*
William Grynes,   ,,   ,,   ,,   ,,
Acton Curvett, *Chief Footman*
James Loveall, *Footman*
Sampson Ashley,   ,,
William Petley,   ,,
Nicholas James,   ,,
Paschal Beard,   ,,
Elias Thomas,   ,,
Henry Spencer, *Farrier*
Edward Goodsall
John Sant, *the Steward's Man*
Ralph Wise, *Groom of the Stables*
Thomas Petley, *Under Farrier*
John Stephens, *the Chaplain's Man*
John Haite, *Groom for the Stranger's Horse*

Thomas Giles, *Groom of the Stables*
Richard Thomas, *Groom of the Hall*
Christopher Wood, *Groom of the Pantry*
George Owen, *Huntsman*
George Vigeon,   ,,
Thomas Grittan, *Groom of the Buttery*
Solomon, *the Bird-Catcher*
Richard Thornton, *the Coachman's Man*
Richard Pickenden, *Postillion*
William Roberts, *Groom*
The Armourer's Man
Ralph Wise, *his Servant*
John Swift, *the Porter's Man*

John Atkins   ⎫
Clement Doory ⎭   *Men to carry wood*

THE LAUNDRY-MAIDS' TABLE

Mrs. Judith Simpton
Mrs. Grace Simpton
Penelope Tutty, *the Lady Margaret's Maid*
Anne Mills, *Dairy-Maid*
Prudence Bucher
Anne Howse
Faith Husband
Elinor Thompson
Goodwife Burton
Grace Robinson, *a Blackamoor*
Goodwife Small
William Lewis, *Porter*

KITCHEN AND SCULLERY

Diggory Dyer
Marfidy Snipt
John Watson
Thomas Harman
Thomas Johnson
John Morockoe, *a Blackamoor*

CHAPTER V

KNOLE IN THE REIGN OF CHARLES I

EDWARD SACKVILLE, 4th Earl *of* Dorset

§ i

HE WRECKAGE of Richard's estates devolved at his death upon s brother Edward, who at that time was travelling in Italy. his Edward Sackville was once to me the embodiment of avalier romance. At the age of thirteen I wrote an enormous ovel about him and his two sons. He had the advantage of arting with Vandyck's portrait in the hall, the flame-coloured oublet, the blue Garter, the characteristic swaggering atti- de, the sword, the love-locks, the key of office painted dang- ng from his hip and the actual key dangling on a ribbon from he frame of the picture—and then the account of his duel ith Lord Bruce, his devotion to Charles I, the plundering aid of Cromwell's soldiers into Knole, the murder of his ounger son by the Roundheads, the picture of the two boys hrowing dice—all this was a source of rich romance to a outhful imagination nourished on *Cyrano* and *The Three Musketeers*. I used to steal up to the attics to examine the old nail-studded trunks from which the Roundheads had broken off the locks. There they were—the visible evidence of the old paper in the Muniment Room, which said, "They have broken open six trunks; in one of them was money; what is lost of it we know not, in regard the keeper of it is from home." There they were, carelessly stacked; on one of them was stabbed the date in big nails, 1623; and there were others, curved to fit the roof of a barouche; of later date these, but all intimate and palpitating to a very ignorant child to whom the centuries meant Thomas or Richard or Edward Sackville; Holbein, Vandyck or Reynolds; farthingale chairs or love-seats. What were dates when the centuries went by generations? The bat- tered trunks were stacked near the entrance to the hiding-place,

which, without the smallest justification save an old candle-
stick and a rope-ladder found therein, I peopled with the
fugitive figures of priests and Royalists. I peeped into the
trunks: they contained only a dusty jumble of broken iron
work, some old books, some bits of hairy plaster fallen from
the ceiling, some numbers of *Punch* for 1850. Nevertheless
there were the gaping holes where the locks had been prised
off the trunks, and the lid forced back upon the hinges by an
impatient hand. Down in the Poets' Parlour, where I lunched
with my grandfather, taciturn unless he happened to crack
one of his little stock-in-trade of jokes, Cromwell's soldiers
had held their Court of Sequestration. The Guard Room was
empty of arms or armour, save for a few pikes and halberds,
because Cromwell's soldiers had taken all the armour away.
The past mingled with the present in constant reminder; and
out in the summer-house, after luncheon, with the bees
blundering among the flowers of the Sunk Garden and the
dragon-flies flashing over the pond, I returned to the immense
ledger in which I was writing my novel, while Grandpapa
retired to his little sitting-room and whittled paper-knives from
the lids of cigar-boxes, and thought about—Heaven knows
what *he* thought about.

Edward Sackville in the big Vandyck was indeed a handsome, rubicund figure, "beautiful, graceful, and vigorous . . .
the vices he had were of the age, which he was not stubborn
enough to resist or to condemn." What these vices were I do
not know; the records of his life make no allusion to them. It
is true that the cause of his duel remains a mystery; Lord
Clarendon knew it, but beyond mentioning that it was fought
on account of a lady, kept his own counsel. It is true also that
his sister-in-law, Lady Anne Clifford, disliked him greatly
and spoke of the malice he had always shown towards her;
but then amicable relationship with Lady Anne was not easily
sustained. On the face of it, his life seems to have been loyal
and honourable: he suffered considerably for the sake of the
cause he had at heart, and his few speeches and letters are full
of reserve and dignity, supported by the facts of his own misfortunes; I do not see what more he could have done to deserve

e adjective staunch. To me at thirteen he was very staunch
d doughty, and one does not willingly go back on one's first
pressions. His wife, too, in the pointed stomacher and the
oes with huge rosettes, governess to the royal children,
ted a public funeral in Westminster Abbey, was another
aunch figure: severe, uncompromising, but impeccable.

The duel with Lord Bruce was fought when Edward Sack-
le was twenty-three years old, at Bergen-op-Zoom in
olland, which so late as 1814 still went by the name of Bruce-
nd. In the Knole Muniment room a paper cover was found
on which was written "The relation of my Lord's duel with
e Lord Bruce," and the following are in all probability the
pers originally contained therein. The "Worthy sir" to
hom the letter is addressed remains anonymous, but was
idently some friend in England:

WORTHY SIR,

As I am not ignorant, so I ought to be sensible of the false
spersions some authorless tongues have laid upon me in the
eports of the unfortunate passage lately happened between the
ord Bruce and myself, which, as they are spread here, so I may
stly fear they reign also where you are. There are but two
ays to resolve doubts of this nature, by oath and by sword.

The first is due to magistrates, and communicable to friends;
he other to such as maliciously slander, and impudently
efend their assertions. Your love, not my merit, assures me
ou hold me your friend; which esteem I am much desirous
o retain. Do me, therefore, the right to understand the truth
f that; and, in my behalf, inform others, who either are or
nay be infected with sinister rumours, much prejudicial to
hat fair opinion I desire to hold amongst all worthy persons;
nd, on the faith of a gentleman, the relation I shall give is
neither more nor less than the bare truth. The enclosed con-
tains the first citation sent me from Paris by a Scottish gentleman, who delivered it me in Derbyshire, at my father-in-law's
house. After it follows my then answer, returned him by the
same bearer. The next is my accomplishment of my first
promise, being a particular assignation of place and weapon,
which I sent by a servant of mine, by post, from Rotterdam,
as soon as I landed there, the receipt of which joined with an

acknowledgement of my fair carriage to the deceased Lord,
testified by the last, which periods the business till we met
Tergose, in Zealand, it being the place allotted for rende
vous; where he [accompanied with one Mr. Crawford, a
English gentleman, for his second, a surgeon, and his ma
arrived with all the speed he could. And there having re
dered himself, I addressed my second, Sir John Heydon,
let him understand that now all following should be done] I
consent, as concerning the terms whereon we should fight, a
also the place. To our seconds we gave power for their appoin
ments, who agreed that we should go to Antwerp, from thenc
to Bergen-op-Zoom, where in the midway a village divide
the States' territories from the Archduke's; and there wa
the destined stage, to the end, that, having ended, he tha
could might presently exempt himself from the justice of th
country, by retiring into the dominion not offended. It wa
further concluded, that in case any should fall or slip, tha
then the combat should cease; and he, whose ill fortune ha
so subjected him, was to acknowledge his life to have been i
the other's hands. But in case one party's sword should break
because that could only chance by hazard, it was agreed tha
the other should take no advantage, but either then be mad
friends, or else, upon even terms, go to it again. Thus thes
conclusions, being by each of them related to his party, were
by us, both approved and assented to. Accordingly we em
barked for Antwerp; and by reason my Lord [as I conceive
because he could not handsomely without danger of discovery
had not paired the sword I sent him to Paris, bringing one o
the same length but twice as broad, my second excepte
against it, and advised me to match my own, and send him the
choice; which I obeyed, it being, you know, the challenger's
privilege to elect his weapon. At the delivery of the swords,
which was performed by Sir John Heydon, it pleased the
Lord Bruce to choose my own; and then, past expectation,
he told him that he found himself so far behind-hand, as a
little of my blood would not serve his turn; and therefore he
was now resolved to have me alone, because he knew [for I
will use his own words] that so worthy a gentleman, and my
friend, could not endure to stand by, and see him do that
which he must, to satisfy himself and his honour. Thereunto
Sir John Heydon replied, that such intentions were bloody
and butcherly, far unfitting so noble a personage, who should

sire to bleed for reputation, not for life; withal adding, he
ought himself injured, being come thus far, now to be pro-
bited from executing those honourable offices he came for.
he Lord Bruce, for answer, only reiterated his former reso-
tion; the which, not for matter, but for manner, so moved
e, as though to my remembrance I had not for a long while
ten more liberally than at dinner; and therefore, unfit for
ch an action [seeing the surgeons hold a wound upon a full
omach much more dangerous than otherwise], I requested
y second to certify him I would presently decide the differ-
ce, and should therefore meet him, on horseback, only
ited on by our surgeons, they being unarmed. Together we
de [but one before the other some twelve score] about two
glish miles; and then Passion, having so weak an enemy to
sail as my direction, easily became victor; and, using his
wer, made me obedient to his commands. I being very mad
th anger the Lord Bruce should thirst after my life with a
nd of assuredness, seeing I had come so far and needlessly
give him leave to regain his lost reputation, I bade him
ght, which with all willingness he quickly granted; and
ere, in a meadow [ankle-deep in the water at least], bidding
rewell to our doublets, in our shirts we began to charge each
her, having afore commanded our surgeons to withdraw
emselves a pretty distance from us; conjuring them besides,
they respected our favour or their own safeties, not to stir,
it suffer us to execute our pleasure; we being fully resolved
od forgive us] to despatch each other by what means we
uld. I made a thrust at my enemy, but was short; and, in
awing back my arm, I received a great wound thereon,
ich I interpreted as a reward for my short shooting; but,
revenge, I pressed in to him, though I then missed him also;
d then received a wound in my right pap, which passed
vel through my body, and almost to my back; and there we
estled for the two greatest and dearest prizes we could ever
pect, trial for honour and life; in which struggling, my hand,
ving but an ordinary glove on it, lost one of her servants,
ough the meanest, which hung by a skin, and, to sight, yet
maineth as before, and I am put in hope one day to recover
e use of it again. But at last breathless, yet keeping our holds,
ere passed on both sides propositions for quitting each
her's sword. But, when Amity was dead, Confidence could
t live, and who should quit first was the question, which on

neither part either would perform; and, re-striving aga
afresh, with a kick and a wrench together I freed my lor
captive weapon, which incontinently levying at his thro
being master still of his, I demanded if he would ask his l
or yield his sword? Both which, though in that immine
danger, he bravely denied to do. Myself being wounded, a
feeling loss of blood, having three conduits running on m
began to make me faint; and he courageously persisting n
to accord to either of my propositions, remembrance of l
former bloody desire, and feeling of my present estate, I stru
at his heart; but, with his avoiding, missed my aim, yet pass
through his body, and, drawing back my sword, repassed
through again through another place, when he cried, "Oh
am slain!" seconding his speech with all the force he had
cast me. But being too weak, after I had defended his assau
I easily became master of him, laying him on his back; wh
being upon him, I redemanded if he would request his li
But it seems he prized it not at so dear a rate to be behold
for it, bravely replying "He scorned it!" which answer of l
was so noble and worthy, as I protest I could not find in n
heart to offer him any more violence, only keeping him dow
till, at length, his surgeon afar off cried out, "He would im
mediately die if his wounds were not stopped!" whereup
I asked, "if he desired his surgeon should come?" which
accepted of; and so being drawn away, I never offered to ta
his sword, accounting it inhumane to rob a dead man, for
I held him to be. This thus ended, I retired to my surgeo
in whose arms, after I had remained awhile for want of bloo
I lost my sight, and withal, as I then thought, my life als
But strong water and his diligence quickly recovered me; wh
I escaped a great danger, for my Lord's surgeon, when nobo
dreamt of it, came full at me with his Lord's sword; and ha
not mine with my sword interposed himself, I had been sla
by those base hands, although my Lord Bruce, weltering
his blood, and past all expectation of life, conformable to
his former carriage, which was undoubtedly noble, cried o
"Rascal, hold thy hand!" So may I prosper, as I have dea
sincerely with you in this relation, which I pray you, with tl
enclosed letter, deliver to my Lord Chamberlain. And so, et

Yours,

EDWARD SACKVILL

LOVAIN, the 8th September, 1613

The citations or letters mentioned above to be enclosed in is account of Mr. Sackville are as follows:

A Monsieur, Monsieur SACKVILLE

I, that am in France, hear how much you attribute to yourself in this time, that I have given the world to ring your raises; and for me the truest almanach to tell you how much suffer. If you call to memory when, as I gave you my hand ast, I told you I reserved the heart for a truer reconciliation, ow be that noble gentleman my love once spoke, and come o him right that would recite the trials you owe your birth nd country, where I am confident your honour gives you the ame courage to do me right that it did to do me wrong. Be naster of your weapons and time; the place wheresoever I vait on you. By doing this you shall shorten revenge, and lear the idle opinion the world hath of both our worths.

ED. BRUCE.

A Monsieur, Monsieur Baron de KINLOSS

As it shall be far from me to seek a quarrel, so will I also be ready to meet with any that is desirous to make trial of my valour, by so fair a course as you require; a witness whereof yourself shall be, who, within a month, shall receive a strict account of time, place and weapon, where you shall find me ready disposed to give honourable satisfaction by him that shall conduct you thither. In the meantime be as secret of the appointment as it seems you are desirous of it.

ED. SACKVILLE.

A Monsieur, Monsieur Baron de KINLOSS

I am at Torgose, a town in Zealand, to give what satisfaction your sword can render you, accompanied with a worthy gentleman for my second, in degree a Knight; and for your coming I will not limit you a peremptory day, but desire you to make a definite and speedy repair, for your own honour and fear of prevention, at which time you shall find me there.

ED. SACKVILLE.

TORGOSE, 10*th August,* 1613

A Monsieur, Monsieur SACKVILLE

I have received your letter by your man, and acknowledg
you have dealt nobly with me, and I come with all possib!
haste to meet you.   E. BRUC!

§ ii

Between this affair and the date of his succession to h:
brother Richard, Edward Sackville was employed on variou
missions: he sat in the House of Commons, he was twice sen
as ambassador to Louis XIII, and he travelled in France an
Italy. He was thus, when he succeeded, an experienced ma:
of thirty-four, and he pursued, uninterruptedly, the sobe
path of office, now Lord Chamberlain, now Lord Privy Seal
now a Commissioner for planting Virginia, always in the con
fidence of the King, and his name affixed to State document:
of the day in noble company. The disgraces and follies of his
predecessors and of his descendants were not his lot, if tha
murderous duel is to be excepted. My flaming Cavalier
flamberge au vent, was in reality a sober and consistent gentleman; loyal, but not impetuous; prejudiced, but not blinded
devoted, but not afraid to speak his mind in criticism; and in
support of this claim I shall presently quote from one of his
speeches in which he argues against a continuance of the Civil
War and pleads for a prompt reconciliation between the King
and his Parliament. His judgment is acute, and his attitude
remarkably sound and broad-minded. Yet at the same time
his devotion to the King was such, that after Charles' execution
Lord Dorset never passed beyond the threshold of his own
door.

There are a few papers at Knole relating to the years before
the war began, and from them one may gather some idea of
the then manner of life, always remembering that Lord Dorset
was much impoverished by the extravagance of his brother.
The total income for the year 1628 from Knole and Sevenoaks
was £100 18s. 6d.—a fifth part of which was derived from the
sale of rabbits. Some details of expenses are given in the
account-books, besides those which I have already given in
connection with the park in the second chapter:

Money spent on the pale in Knole Park for one year
(*£8 9s. 6d.*) *as follows:*

	£	s.	d.
For filling, cleaning, and making six loads of pale rails, posts, and shores, two men	0	8	0
Setting up panels of pales, blown down by the wind against Riverhill, 10d. day each man	0	5	0
Paid a labourer for spreading the mole hills in the meads and for killing moles	0	4	3

The steward of Sevenoaks was paid ten shillings a year, the bailiff at Sevenoaks £10, the steward of Seal £2 10s., the bailiff of Seal £4.

	£	s.	d.
Four hundred nails for the pales	0	2	0
Paid for setting up pales at mock-beech gate	0	0	8
Paid toward repairing the market cross in Sevenoaks	6	8	4

Portions of the park, such as were not already under cultivation of hops, were leased out to farmers for grazing:

	£	s.	d.
The joistment[1] of Knole Park, May 1629.			
Of William Bloom for 3 yearlings	1	0	0
Of George Dennis for keeping 20 runts[2]	0	13	4
Of Richard Wicking for his kines' pasture	0	13	0
Of Richard Fletcher for summering 2 colts	0	16	0

There were other sources of revenue. Letters patent granted an imposition of 4s. per chaldron on all coal exported, to be divided among the Earl of Dorset, the Earl of Holland, and Sir Job Harby:

COAL IMPOSITIONS

	£	s.	d.
6th May, 1634	4312	13	0
Deduction for expenses	507	11	4
Rest to be divided into thirds	3805	1	8

[1] Joistment: the feeding of cattle in a common pasture for a stipulated fee.
[2] Runts: young ox or cow.

That is to say, Dorset's share would be £1268 7s. 8d., or mo
than £10,000 of modern money.

He obtained also £100 a year by devising to Richard Gunn
and William Blagrave for four and a half years a piece of lan
at the lower end of Salisbury Court, Fleet Street, 140 feet i
length and 42 feet in breadth, on condition that they shoul
at their own expense put up a play-house. What would be th
rent of such a piece of land now in Fleet Street? Certainly n
£100.

In spite of the fact that he complained constantly of hi
reduced income, Lord Dorset added considerably to the park
He obtained a long lease of Seal Chart, and "all woods an
under-woods of the waste or common of the Manors of Sea
and Kemsing, viz., upon Rumshott Common, Riverhill Com
mon, Hubbard Hill Common, and Westwood Common . .
in all at least 500 acres."

More entertaining is the acquisition of an overseas estate—
no less than that part of the east coast of America which to-da
includes New York, Boston, and Philadelphia. Those littl
manors in the neighbourhood of Sevenoaks, those 500 acre
of common land, dwindle suddenly beside this formidabl
tenure. "An island called Sandy [Hook]" the petition casuall
begins:

An island called Sandy, lying near the continent of America,
in the height of 44 degrees, was lately discovered by one Rose,
late master of a ship, who suffered shipwreck, and, finding no
inhabitants, took possession. The Earl of Dorset prays a grant
of the said island for thirty-one years, and that none may
adventure thither but such as petitioner shall licence.

A second petition takes one's breath away with its
magnificent insolence:

The Earl of Dorset to the King. Certain islands on the
south of New England, viz: Long Island, Cole Island, Sandy
Point, Hell Gates, Martin's [? Martha's] Vineyard, Elizabeth
Islands, Block Island, with other islands near thereunto, were
lately discovered by some of your Majesty's subjects and are
not yet inhabited by Christians. Prays a grant thereof with

ke powers of government as have been granted for other
lantations in America.

Underneath this is scribbled:

Reference to the Attorney-General to prepare a grant.
Vhitehall, 20th Dec., 1637.

One would wish to evoke for a brief hour the spectres of
hose of his Majesty's subjects who found these localities
uninhabited by Christians.

Returning to Knole after this seems paltry; yet even there
ord Dorset was conducting his affairs on a proportionately
arge scale. He said himself that he spent £40,000 after his
on's marriage, and one can believe it when one reads a
ample of the bill of fare provided for a banquet. At the top is
written:

To perfume the room often in the meal with orange flower
water upon a hot pan. To have fresh bowls in every corner and
flowers tied upon them, and sweet briar, stock, gilly-flowers,
pinks, wallflowers and any other sweet flowers in glasses and
pots in every window and chimney.

BANQUET *at* KNOLE *3rd July* 1636

1 Rice Pottage	17 Tenches, boiled
2 Barley broth	18 Crabs
3 Buttered pickrell	19 Tench pie
4 Buttered and burned eggs	20 Venison pasty of a Doe
5 Boiled teats	21 Sawns (2)
6 Roast tongues	22 Herons (3)
7 Bream	23 Cold lamb
8 Perches	24 Custard
9 Chine of Veal roast	25 Venison, boiled
10 Hash of mutton with Anchovies	26 Potatoes, stewed
	27 Gr. salad
11 Gr. Pike	28 Redeeve [*sic*] pie, hot
12 Fish chuits [*sic*]	29 Almond pudding
13 Roast venison, in blood	30 Made dishes
14 Capons (2)	31 Boiled salad
15 Wild ducks (3)	32 Pig, whole
16 Salmon whole, hot	33 Rabbits

Another Menu

1 Jelly of Tench, Jelly of Hartshorn	17 Seagulls (6)
2 White Gingerbread	18 Ham of bacon
3 Puits [peewits]	19 Sturgeon
4 Curlew	20 Lark pie
5 Ruffes [sic]	21 Lobster pie
6 Fried perches	22 Crayfishes (3 doz.)
7 Fried Eels	23 Dried tongues
8 Skirret Pie	24 Anchovies
9 Larks (3 doz.)	25 Hartechocks [artichokes]
10 Plovers (12)	26 Peas
11 Teals (12)	27 Fool
12 Fried Pickrell	28 Second porridge
13 Fried tench	29 Reddeeve pie [sic]
14 Salmon soused	30 Cherry tart
15 Soused eel	31 Laid tart
16 Escanechia [sic]	32 Carps (2)
	33 Polony sasag [sic]

There is also a list of "household stuff" dated the year of Lord Dorset's succession.

" 𝕬 𝕹ote

of household stuff sent by SYMONDES to KNOLE the 28th of July 1624."

Packed up in a fardel, viz.: in ye black bed chamber

IMPRIMIS. A fustian down bed, bolster and a pair of pillows, a pair of Spanish blankets, 5 curtains of crimson and white taffeta, the valance to it of white satin embroidered with crimson and white silk and a deep fringe suitable; a test and tester of white satin suitable to the valance. A white rug. All these first packed up in 2 sheets and then packed in a white and black rug and an old blanket.

Packed in another fardel, viz.: next ye chapel chamber

IT: A feather bed and bolster, a pair of down pillows, 2 mattrasses, 5 curtains and valances of yellow cotton trimmed with blue and yellow silk fringes and lace suitable, a tester to it suitable, a cushion case of yellow satin, a pair of blankets to wrap these things in, there is also in the fardel a yellow rug, and a white and black rug.

ye black bed-chamber   IT: Two bedsteads whereof one of them is gilt, which with the posts, tests, curtains, etc., are in all 11 parcels whereof 4 are matted.

ye black bed-chamber   IT: Packed up in mats 2 high stools, 2 low stools, and a footstool of cloth of tissue and chair suitable.

ext ye Chaplain's chamber   IT: There goes a yellow satin chair and 3 stools, suitable with their buckram covers to them. All the above written came from Croxall.

IT: Packed in mats my lady's coach of cloth of silver, and 2 low stools that came from Croxall, and a said bag, wherein are 9 cups of crimson damask laid with silver parchment lace, and 6 gilt cups for my lord's couch bed and canopy, and 8 gilt cups for the bed that came from Croxall.

IT: In a wicker trunk, 2 brass branches for a dozen lights apiece; and 2 single branches with bosses and bucks heads to them, also a wooden box with screws for the said 2 bedsteads, a dozen of spiggots to draw wine and beer, a bundle of marsh mallow roots, and 2 papers of almonds.

IT: A round wicker basket, wherein are 9 dozen of pewter vessels of 9 sorts or sizes.

IT: 4 back stools of crimson and yellow stuff with silk fringe suitable, covered with yellow baize.

IT: 6 pairs of mats to mat chambers with gt 30 yards apiece.

IT: 2 walnut tree tables to draw out at both ends with their frames of the same.

IT: A round table and its frame.

Next ye Chaplain's chamber   IT: 2 green broad cloth chairs, covered over, laced, and set with green silk frin and a back stool suitable, covered with gre buckram.

IT: A box containing 3 dozen of Veni glasses.

IT: A basket wherein are 20 dozen of map trenchers.

And finally, for I fear lest the detailing of these old pape should grow wearisome, there is a letter which so well illu trates the humour, the coarseness, and the difficulties of li at that time, that I make no apology for including it:

𝔏etter

from ELIZA COPE to her sister the COUNTESS *of* BATH

19th Jan. 1639. BREWERN

DEAR SISTER,

I am glad to hear of your jollity. I could wish myself wit you a little while sometimes. I have played at cards 4 or times this Christmas myself, after supper, which makes m think I begin to turn gallant now. Some of my neighbours pu a compliment upon me this Christmas, and told me the ol Lady Cope would never be dead so long as I was alive, the liked their entertainment so well, when my gilt bowl wen round amongst them, which saying pleased me very well, fo she was a discreet woman and worthy the imitating. I am a well pleased to see my little man make legs and dance a gal liard, as if I had seen the mask at Court. I am glad you go well home for we have had extreme ill weather almost eve since you went, but now I will take the benefit of this frost to go visit some of my neighbours on foot to-morrow about seven miles off, but I will have a coach and 6 horses within a call against I am weary. You know the old saying, it is good going on foot with a horse in the hand.

Commend my service to your lord, and wishing to hear you were puking a-mornings I bid ye good-night in haste.

Your faithful sister,

ELIZA COPE.

§ iii

On the approach of civil war there could be no doubt on which side the Earl of Dorset would range himself. He had been for many years closely connected with both the King and Henrietta Maria, and Lady Dorset stood in a yet more intimate relationship to the King and Queen as governess to their children. Since 1630, the date of the birth of Charles II, she had held this position, and from this little anecdote it may be judged that she was not so severe a preceptress as her portrait might lead one to suppose:

Charles II, when a child, was weak in the legs, and ordered to wear steel boots. Their weight so annoyed him that he pined till recreation became labour—an old Rocker took off the steel boots and concealed them: promising the Countess of Dorset, who was Charles' governess, that he would take any blame for the act on himself. Soon afterwards, the King, Charles I, coming into the nursery, and seeing the boy's legs without the boots, angrily demanded who had done it. "It was I, Sir," said the Rocker, "who had the honour some thirty years since to attend on your Highness in your infancy, when you had the same infirmity wherewith now the Prince, your very own son, is troubled—and then the Lady Cary, afterwards Countess of Monmouth, commanded your steel boots to be taken off, who, blessed be God, since have gathered strength and arrived at a good stature.

It is no small tribute to Lady Dorset's integrity that after the outbreak of war she should have been continued in her office by Parliament.

I have in my own possession a receipt signed by her for £125 for salary and expenses, 1641.

War became imminent:

"the citizens grow very tumultous and flock by troops daily to the Parliament . . . they never cease yawling and crying "No Bishops, no Bishops!" My lord of Dorset is appointed to command the train-bands, but the citizens slight muskets charged with powder. I myself saw the Guard attempt to drive the citizens forth, but the citizens blustered at them and

would not stir. I saw and heard my Lord of Dorset entrea
them with his hat in his hand and yet the scoundrels woul
not move."

It is clear from contemporary documents that Lord Dorse
was preparing to take an active part. He did, in fact, raise
troop which he equipped at his own expense, and with whic
he joined the King at York. But the old inventories give a lis
of residue arms and armour indicating a quantity originall
more numerous than would be necessary to equip a smal
troop; the whole house must have been rifled to produce thes
weapons, all carefully listed, whether complete or incomplete
serviceable or not serviceable, old-fashioned or up to date
One can read between the lines of the list the anxiety tha
nothing should be omitted which could possibly be pressec
into the service of the King. Among the armour at Knole a
this date must have been the fine suit of tilting armour,
formerly the property of the old Lord Treasurer, and now ir
the Wallace Collection, described as "a complete suit of
armour . . . richly decorated by bands and bordering, deeply
etched and partly gilt with a scroll design . . . the plain surfaces
oxidised to a rich russet-brown known in inventories of the
period as purple armour." This suit, which is one of the gems
of the Wallace Collection, had been made in 1575 by Jacob
Topp or Jacobi for Sir Thomas Sackville.

"An Inventory

of such arms as are now remaining in the armoury at Knole
belonging to the Rt. Hon. EDWARD EARL of DORSET,
first the horseman's arms & necessaries belonging to them:"

Cornets for Horses	2
Curasiers arms gilt	2
Curasiers arms plain	31
White tilting armour	3
A baryears Armour gorget and gauntlet wanting	1
Sham front for tilting Run plates for barryers	1
Plated saddles suitable to the gilt arms and furniture rotten	2

Old russet saddles trimmed with red leather and furniture defaulting	12
Old russet and black saddles	12
Black leather saddles with all furniture bits excepted	2
Old French pistols, whereof four have locks the other 9 have none and double moulds to them	13
Swords	14
Horn flasks	49
Whereof an old damask one cornered with velvet and many not serviceable	
Slight arms, back and breast 2 gorgets only to them	13

Arms and other necessaries for foot men

One engraven target	1
Partisan rolled with red velvet and nailed with gilt nails and damasked with gold	1
Partisans Damasked with Silver and the Cat on them [the Cat, *i.e.* the leopard]	4
Corslets with back breast cases and headpieces	138
Spanish picks and English picks with Spanish heads whereof 4 are broken	151
Comb head pieces	70
Old Spanish morions	50
Halberts	7
Bits	6
Full muskets complete	76
Bastard muskets	56
Muskets imperfect	4
Noulds to the muskets	2
New Rests	64
Old Rests	7
Bandeliers	36
Barrels of match wanting 16 bundles	2

(Signed) DORSET. *Jan.* 1641

It was not very long before the Parliamentarians got wind of this hoard, and in August 1642 three troops of horse under the command of one Cornell Sandys rode into Kent, invaded Knole, took prisoner a Sir John Sackville whom they found

in charge there, did a certain amount of rough damage, a⸱
carried off the contents of the armoury to London. T⸱
proceedings were thus officially reported:

Some SPECIAL & REMARKABLE PASSAGES

from both houses of PARLIAMENT *since Monday* 15*th of Aug. t⸱*
Friday the 19*th* 1642.

Upon Saturday night last, the Lord General having i⸱
formation of a great quantity of Arms of the Earl of Dorse⸱
at his house at Sevenoaks, in Kent, in the custody of Sir Jo⸱
Sackville, which were to be disposed of by him to arm a gre⸱
number of the malignant party of that County, to go to Yo⸱
to assist his Majesty; called a Council of War, to consid⸱
of the same, and about 12 of the clock at night sent out⸱
troops of Horse into Kent to seize upon the said Arms; whi⸱
they did accordingly on the Sunday following; and on th⸱
Monday brought the same to London and Sir John Sackvil⸱
prisoner, there being complete arms for 500 or 600 men.

Despite the outcry of plaintive indignation which went u⸱
from Knole, the House of Lords report proves that their con⸱
duct towards Lord Dorset over the incident was fair, lenien⸱
and even generous:

That the Arms of the Earl of Dorset which were at Kno⸱
House, are brought to Town, to be kept from being made us⸱
of against the Parliament,

and therefore this House ordered,

That such as are rich Arms shall not be made use of, but kep⸱
safely for the Earl of Dorset; but such as are fit to be made us⸱
of for the service of the Kingdom are to be employed; a⸱
Inventory to be taken, and money to be given to the Earl o⸱
Dorset in satisfaction thereof.

Thus ran the official reports; but Knole, astonished
aggrieved, and outraged, drew up a fuller list of injuries. I⸱
was the first time rude voices had ever echoed within those
venerable walls or rude hands rummaged among the sacred
possessions, the first time that orders had been issued there

another than the master. The Parliament men had entered
th arrogance, spoken with authority, gone beyond their
rrant, and ransacked wantonly—from what motive but
ntonness could they have taken the plumes from the bed-
ster or the cushions from his Lordship's own room? or
oilt the oil in the Painter's Chamber? or, indeed, broken
rty locks, unless to overcome such slight resistance in an
nnecessarily high-handed manner? No doubt the novelty of
e experience turned their heads. Rhetorically they were the
presentatives of the English Parliament, that sober and
nacious senate, as stubborn now as at Runnymede, but in
:ivate life they were men, however insignificant hitherto to
ord Dorset, men who, when he passed with a swagger, mur-
ured dully beneath their reluctant deference. The moment
hen, cantering up over the crest of the hill, they first saw the
rey forbidding walls and drew rein before the massive door,
eir horses' bits jingling and the restive hoofs pawing at the
ravel, must indeed have been an experience. Likewise, to
ing their spurs on the paving-stones of the courtyards, to
ass from room to room followed by a protesting and im-
otent steward, to stare at the pictures, to lounge on the velvet
hairs, to set out their ink and paper on the solid table of the
arlour and to draw up their indictment. It was August; the
ose planted beneath the window of a Stuart King to com-
nemorate his visit was covered with its little white blossoms;
he turf was smooth and green; the flowers were bright under
he young apple-trees in the orchard; the beeches and chest-
nuts were deep and heavy with the fullness of summer. The
usterity of the Roundheads surely stiffened in the soft summer
paciousness of Knole. The owner was absent: they had only
his new portrait to gaze at, with scorn of his brilliant doublet
and his curling hair.

All things considered, I think that they showed com-
mendable restraint in their behaviour:

The hurt done at KNOLE HOUSE *the* 14 *Day of August* 1642
by the COMPANY OF HORSEMEN *brought by* CORNELL SANDYS:

There are above forty stock locks and plated locks broken,
which to make good will cost £10.

There is of gold branches belonging to the couch in the ri
gallery as much cut away as will not be made good for £40.

And in my Lord's chamber 12 long cushion-cases er
broidered with satin and gold, and the plumes upon the be
tester, to ye value of £30.

They have broken open six trunks; in one of them w
money; what is lost of it we know not, in regard the keeper
it is from home. They have spoiled in the Painter's Chamb
his oil, and other wrongs there to the value of £40.

They have broke into Sir John his Granary and have take
of his oats and peas, to the quantity of three or four quarte
£4.

The arms they have wholly taken away, there being fiv
waggon-loads of them.

Nor was this the last time that the Parliamentarians can
to Knole. Three years after these events Cromwell's com
missioners were installed there as the headquarters of th
Court of Sequestration for Kent, and held their sessions i
the Poets' Parlour, when the Sackvilles were, for a short time
deprived of the property. On this occasion there is no recor
of any definite damage to the contents of the house, althoug
a House of Commons notice for January 1645 ordered tha
"two-thirds of the goods and estates of the Earl of Dorset nc
exceeding the sum of £500 now at Knole in the county o
Kent, and lately discovered there, shall be employed for th
use of the garrison at Dover Castle, towards the pay of thei
arrears."

Among the papers in the Muniment Room I find a lette
of a later date from Sir Kenelm Digby to Lord Dorset, refer
ring to some stolen pictures which he has been endeavourin
to trace in Paris, and recommending to Lord Dorset a certai
M. La Fontaine for "the much pains and running about h
hath used," suggesting that he should be rewarded with 20s
and recommended to good customers to sell his "powders anc
cigeours." I wonder inevitably whether the loss of these pic
tures had been due to any action of Cromwell or his com
missioners? Sir Kenelm's letter, which is long, rambling, and
rather illegible, does not make any mention of the cause or
date of the disappearance. Sir Kenelm is himself of greater

erest, perhaps, than his letter or the pictures. An intimate
end of Lord Dorset's, the author of several housewifely little
atises, such as *The Closet of Sir Kenelm Digby* and *Choice
d Experimental Receipts*, he was incidentally the husband of
at Venetia Stanley whose lover Richard Sackville had been.

has, I may mention, been suggested that Edward Sack-
le, not Richard, was the lover of Lady Digby; and having
gard to what I know of Sir Kenelm's character I should think
not inconsistent, even if this were so, that he should remain
a most friendly terms with the former lover of his wife. He
d, after all, not scrupled to sue Lord Dorset, whether
chard or Edward, for the continuance after marriage of
ady Digby's pension of £500 a year.) Sir Kenelm's portrait
Vandyck is at Knole in the Poets' Parlour; he is a chubby
tle man, with a fat outspread hand, and dimples in the place
knuckles. At one period of the Civil War he suffered im-
isonment, when Lord Dorset, wishing to beguile his friend's
dium, advised him to read the recently published *Religio
Iedici* of Sir Thomas Browne: Sir Kenelm took his advice,
d was so much impressed as to embody his observations in a
ng letter to Lord Dorset, which was subsequently printed
643) by "R. C. for Daniel Frere, to be sold at his shop at
e Red Bull in Little Britain." I happen to possess the first
litions of the *Religio Medici* and the little companion
olume of Sir Kenelm's *Observations*: the former is heavily
cored or commented by some appreciative reader, and atten-
on is called in the margin to favourite passages by the
rawing of a tiny hand with pointing finger, the wrist en-
ircled by a cuff of *point de Venise*. Sir Kenelm esteemed his
riend's taste, and the "spirit and smartness" of the author,
vho set out upon his task so excellently poised with a happy
emper. Towards the end of his discourse Sir Kenelm quite
oses his sense of proportion in his enthusiasm over Lord
Dorset's discernment, and exclaims:

Tu regere imperio populos [Sackville] *memento,*

nd concludes by dating his letter "the 22nd [I think I may
ay the 23rd, for I am sure it is morning, and I think it is day]

of December 1642," thus proving that he has sat up all ni
in prison with Sir Thomas Browne—and who in this gene
tion could with truth make such a boast?

§ iv

More tragical events than the desecration of his house
the imprisonment of his chubby friend marked for Lo
Dorset the progress of the Civil War. His eldest son, Lo
Buckhurst, was early taken prisoner at Miles End Gre
with Lord Middlesex and that same Sir Kenelm Digby. H
younger son, Edward, was also taken prisoner at Kidlingto
near Oxford, and murdered in cold blood by a Roundhea
soldier shortly after, at Abingdon. When I first wrote th
book I knew nothing further about this Edward Sackvi
except that he was knighted at an early age, was reported
be "a good chymist," and was deplored in an obituary poe
as being

> . . . . *a lamp that had consumed*
> *Scarce half its oil, yet the whole place perfumed*
> *Wherein he lived, or did in kindness come,*
> *As if composed of precious Balsamum,*

and as being to his friends

> *that lost in losing him,*
> *An eye, a tongue, a hand, or some choice limb.*

It now appears, however, that the well-known picture i
the National Portrait Gallery of the Duke of Monmouth
illegitimate son of Charles II, may not be the Duke of Mon
mouth at all, but Edward Sackville. There has been a grea
deal of argument and correspondence on this problem whic
is not yet resolved. I will not go into all the details here—the
would make a whole mystery historical novel—but will refe
anyone interested to an article published in *Country Life*
July 8, 1949, and a subsequent letter in *Country Life*, October 8
1953, and also to a lot of letters I now have in my own pos
session. I don't know what to think about it myself. Is tha
handsome young head, lying on a pillow, with the shee

awn up close to the chin, James Duke of Monmouth or is it
Edward Sackville? I wish I knew.

The author of the obituary poem on Edward Sackville,
Aurelian Townsend, contributed also to the Knole papers a
set of verses on the death of Charles I. "It is a shame," he
exclaims,

> those that can write in verse,
> Quite cover not with elegies his hearse,

and asks:

> Where are the learned sisters, whose full breast
> Was wont to yield such store of milk, unpressed?

The King, he says, was

> . . . . pious, temperate, and grave,
> Just, gentle, constant, merciful, and brave.
> All this, and more, he was not pleased to be,
> Without the woman's virtue, Chastity,

most unlike Solomon, who was wise, yet

> . . . . did incline
> To worship idols, for a concubine.

Lord Dorset himself took an active part in the fighting. At
Edgehill he recaptured the Royal Standard which had been
lost to the enemy, and to his answer during the same battle
James II later testified:

> The old Earl of Dorset, at Edgehill [he wrote], being com-
> manded by the King my father to carry the Prince [Charles II]
> and myself up a hill out of the battle, refused to do it, and said
> he would not be thought a coward for ever a King's son in
> Christendom.

I think also that one of his speeches is worth printing, made
at the Council table in reply to one of Lord Bristol's urging the
continuance of the war. It is honest, enlightened, bold, and,
considering his personal grievances, very dignified:

> The Earl of Bristol has delivered his opinion; and, my turn
> being next to speak, I shall, with the like integrity, give your

Lordships an account of my sentiments in this great and im portant business. I shall not, as young students do in t schools, *argumentandi gratia*, repugn my Lord of Bristo tenets; but because my conscience tells me they are not orth dox, nor consonant to the disposition of the Commonweal which, languishing with a tedious sickness, must be re covered by gentle and easy medicines in consideration of weakness rather than by violent vomits, or any other kind compelling physic. Not that I shall absolutely labour to refu my Lord's opinion, but justly deliver my own, which, bei contrary to his, may appear an express contradiction of which indeed it is not; peace, and that a sudden one, being necessary betwixt his Majesty and his Parliament as light requisite for the production of the day, or heat to cheri from above all inferior bodies; this division betwixt Majesty and his Parliament being as if [by miracle] the su should be separated from his beams, and divided from proper essence. I would not, my Lords, be ready to embrac a peace that would be more disadvantageous to us than t present war, which, as the Earl of Bristol says, "would destr our estates and families." The Parliament declares on against delinquents; such as they conjecture have mi counselled his Majesty, and be the authors of these tumults the Commonwealth. But these declarations of theirs, exce such crimes can be proved against them, are of no validit The Parliament will do nothing unjustly, nor condemn t innocent; and certainly innocent men had not need to fe to appear before any judges whatsoever. And he, who sha for any cause prefer his own private good before the pub utility, is but an ill son of the Commonwealth. *For my par cular, in these wars I have suffered as much as any; my hou hath been searched, my arms taken thence, and my son-and-he committed to prison. Yet I shall wave these discourtesies, becau I know there was a necessity it should be so; and as the darli business of the kingdom, the honour and prosperity of the Kin study to reconcile all these differences betwixt his Majesty an his Parliament; and so to reconcile them, that they shall no w prejudice his royal prerogative; of which I believe the Parliame being a loyal defender* [knowing the subject's property depen on it; for, if sovereigns cannot enjoy their rights, their subjec cannot] will never endeavour to be infringed; so that, doubts and jealousies were taken away by a fair treaty betwe

is Majesty and the Parliament, no doubt a means might be
devised to rectify these differences—the honour of the King,
the estate of us his followers and counsellors, the privileges
of Parliament, and property of the subject, be infallibly
reserved in safety: and neither the King stoop in this to his
subjects, nor the subjects be deprived of their just liberties by
the King. And whereas my Lord of Bristol observes, "that in
Spain very few civil dissensions arise, because the subjects
are truly subjects, and the Sovereign truly a Sovereign"; that
is, as I understand, the subjects are scarcely removed a degree
from slaves, nor the Sovereign from a tyrant; here in England
the subjects have, by long-received liberties granted to our
ancestors by their Kings, made their freedom resolve into a
second nature; and neither is it safe for our Kings to strive
to introduce the Spanish Government upon these free-born
nations, nor just for the people to suffer that Government to
be imposed upon them, which I am certain his Majesty's
goodness never intended. And whereas my Lord of Bristol
intimates the strength and bravery of our army as an induce-
ment to the continuation of these wars, which he promises
himself will produce a fair and happy peace; in this I am
utterly repugnant to his opinion; for, grant that we have an
army of gallant and able men, which, indeed, cannot be denied,
yet we have infinite disadvantages on our side, the Parliament
having double our number, and surely [though our enemies]
persons of as much bravery, nay, and sure to be daily supported, when any of their number fails; a benefit which we
cannot bestow, they having the most populous part of the
kingdom at their devotion; all, or most, of the cities, considerable towns and ports, together with the mainest pillar of
the kingdom's safety, the sea, at their command, and the navy;
and, which is most material of all, an inexhaustible Indies of
money to pay their soldiers, out of the liberal contributions
of coin and plate sent in by people of all conditions, who
account the Parliament's cause their cause, and so think themselves engaged to part with the uttermost penny of their
estates in their defence, whom they esteem the patriots of
their liberties. These strengths of theirs and the defects of
ours considered, I conclude it necessary for all our safeties,
and the good of the whole Commonwealth, to beseech his
Majesty to take some present order for a treaty of peace
betwixt himself and his high court of Parliament, who, I

believe, are so loyal and obedient to his sacred Majesty, tha
they will propound nothing that shall be prejudicial to hi
royal prerogative, or repugnant to their fidelity and duty.

It is, of course, not at all to my purpose to follow the cours
of the Civil War, but only to say that after the execution o
the King Lord Dorset made a vow, which he is believed to hav
kept, that he would never again stir out of his house until h
should be carried out of it in his coffin. He did not, in poin
of fact, survive the King by very many years, but died in 165
and was buried at Withyham.

In Francis Bacon's will, drawn up *circa* 1625, occurs th
following legacy:

"I give unto the right honourable my noble friend Edward
Earl of Dorset, my ring with the crushed diamond which the
King that now is gave to me when he was prince."

Where is that ring now? and what on earth is a crushed
diamond?

CHAPTER VI

KNOLE IN THE REIGN OF CHARLES II

CHARLES, 6th Earl *of* Dorset

§ i

DWARD SACKVILLE was succeeded by his son Richard, married Lady Frances Cranfield, a considerable heiress, who, on the ath of her brother, inherited the fortune and property of eir father, Lionel Cranfield, Earl of Middlesex, sometime reasurer to James I. I mention this marriage especially, cause it brought to the Sackvilles the house called Copt all in Essex and its contents, which included much of the est furniture now at Knole, some of the tapestry, the many rtraits of the Cranfields by Mytens and Dobson, the series historical portraits in the Brown Gallery, and the Mytens pies of Raphael's cartoons. There are a number of receipts Knole to no less than six different carriers, for wagon-loads effects removed from Copt Hall to Knole at the cost of 5s. per load. From Copt Hall also came the carved stone ield now in the Stone Court on the roof of the Great Hall. he Copt Hall estate was sold in 1701 for the approximate m of twenty thousand pounds. The draft of the marriage ttlement is at Knole:

nuary 25th, 1640

The Earl of Middlesex is to assure ten thousand pounds to e Earl of Dorset in marriage with the Lady Frances Cranfield the Lord Buckhurst to be paid in times and manner llowing:
He is to retain the money in his hands, paying yearly to the ung couple towards their maintenance by equal portions at ichaelmas and our Lady Day £800 per annum until a inture be made of £1500 per annum, by the Lord Buckhurst ining with the Earl of Dorset when he shall come to full age. And if the Lord Buckhurst [which God forbid] shall decease

before the said lady, or a jointure so made, then the t
thousand pound shall be the sole use of the said lady. But
the said lady [which God forbid] should die before the Lo
Buckhurst without children, the said portion or so much sh
remain not laid out by consent of the Earl of Dorset in pu
chasing in lands or leases, shall be paid to the said Earl
Dorset.

And in the same connection there are some notes fro
Edward, Lord Dorset to Lord Middlesex, one written "th
Thursday morning at 5 of the clock," apologizing for t
"bad character" which Lord Middlesex must decipher—an
indeed the writing is all but illegible—but he is obliged
write as he must go presently into Kent to dispose son
bargains and sales.

No particular interest attaches to Richard Sackville, sa
that he translated *Le Cid* into English verse and wrote a poe
on Ben Jonson, but there are at Knole some memorandu
books in his handwriting (between 1660 and 1670) which a
worth quoting, I think, for the following illuminati
extracts:

From the DIARY of SERVANTS' faults

	£	s.
Henry Mattock, for scolding to extremity on Sunday without cause	o	o
William Loe, for running out of doors from Morning till Midnight without leave	o	2
Richard Meadowes, for being absent when my Lord came home late, and making a headless excuse	o	o
Henry Mattock, for not doing what he is bidden	o	1
And 3d. a day till he does from this day.		
Henry Mattock, for disposing of my cast linen without my order	o	o
Robert Verrell, for giving away my money	o	o
Henry Mattock, for speaking against going to Knole	o	o

Verrell to pay for not burning the brakes out of
the Wilderness, 3d. per week out of his week's
wages of 5s. for forty-two weeks.

There are various other notes in the same books: Thomas
￼rter, going to Knole, was to have five shillings a week
￼ard-wages; and, judging from the following, Lord Dorset
￼idently could not wholly trust his memory unaided: "My
￼rench shot-bag; an hammer, and some playthings for Tom,
￼ bone knife, etc. A great Iron chafing-dish, or a fire-pan to
￼t it upon." And again, "A silver porringer for little Tom."
Another day he notes:

Old lead cast at Knole for the two turrets weighing 1500 lbs.
￼ld lead cast for the cistern weighing 1200 lbs. Sold 13th
￼ug. 1662 to Edmund Giles and Edward Bourne the Advow-
￼n of the Rectory and Parsonage of Tooting in Surrey for
￼n £100 and paid my wife.

There is also a receipt:

￼ov. 14, 1671. Rec̃ᵈ of the Right Hon. RICHARD Earl of
￼ORSET, in full of all wages bills and accounts whatsoever
￼rom ye beginning of ye World to this day ye full sum of five
￼ounds seven shillings and sixpence I say rec'd by JOHN WALL
￼ROVE.

There is also a letter in a childish writing, which shows
￼Richard in an amiable light as a protector of the young. I have
￼o idea who Thomas Ireland was, nor his enimy Margery, nor
he bad William, but here is the letter to speak for itself:

This is for the right Honᵇˡᵉ Earle of Dorsett att Knoll.
                                        Aug. 15, 1676. *Knoll.*

MY LORD
    I am glad your Lordship is come home; for to take my part,
against my enimy Margery for I did want your Lordship for
to take my part, for she does abuse me most sadly and bet me,
and call my Mother whore, and me Bastard; and whore-master,
and Roach belly, which affrount I can not stand it, I hop your
Lordship will bete her, because I am to little for to bet her,
and I desire your Lordship to bet William, because he threw
me downe against the stones, and had allmost broken my head,
for there is a great boump in my head still, for I thought I
should nevr rise again soe I rest
                Your Lordships very humble servant
                                        THOMAS IRELAND.

§ ii

This Richard Sackville and Frances Cranfield had seve
sons and six daughters. There are some delightful portraits
the little girls at Knole, one in particular of Lady Anne an
Lady Frances, painted in a garden, leading a squirrel on
blue ribbon, and in the chapel at Withyham there is an elab
orate monument to commemorate the youngest son, Thoma
no doubt the "little Tom" for whom the playthings and th
silver porringer were to be remembered. The monument bea
the following inscription:

> *Stand not amaz'd [Reader] to see us shed*
> *From drowned eyes vain offerings to ye dead*
> *For he whose sacred ashes here doth lie*
> *Was the great hopes of all our family.*
> *To blaze whose virtues is but to detract*
> *From them, for in them none can be exact.*
> *So grave and hopeful was his youth,*
> *So dear a friend to piety and truth,*
> *He scarce knew sin, but what curst nature gave,*
> *And yet grim death hath snatch'd him to his grave.*
> *He never to his Parents was unkind*
> *But in his early leaving them behind,*
> *And since hath left us and for e'er is gone*
> *What Mother would not weep for such a Son—*
> *May this fair Monument then never fade,*
> *Or be by blasting time or age decay'd.*
> *That the succeeding times to all may tell*
> *Here lieth one that liv'd and died well—*
> *Here lies the thirteenth child and seventh son*
> *Who in his thirteenth year his race had run.*
>
> THOMAS SACKVILLE.

Of the other children, save of the eldest, there is no record,
or none worth quoting: many of them died, as happened with
such pitiable frequency, at a very early age: Lionel, aged
three; Catherine, aged one: Cranfield, aged fourteen days;
Elizabeth, aged two years; Anne, aged three. The eldest son,

wever, is one of the most jovial and debonair figures in the
ole portrait-gallery, Charles, the sixth Earl—let us call him
e Restoration Earl—the jolly, loose-living, magnificent
æcenas, "during the whole of his life the patron of men of
nius and the dupe of women, and bountiful beyond measure
both." He furnished Knole with silver, and peopled it with
ets and courtesans; he left us the Poets' Parlour, rich with
emories of Pope and Dryden, Prior and Shadwell, D'Urfey
d Killigrew; he left us the silver and ebony stands on which
was in the habit in hours of relaxation of placing his cum-
rsome periwig; he left us his portraits, both as the bewigged
d be-ribboned courtier, and as the host, wrapped in a loose
be, a turban twisted round his head; he left us his gay and
tificial stanzas to Chloris and Dorinda, and his rousing little
ng written on the eve of a naval engagement. He is not, per-
ps, a very admirable figure. He was not above trafficking in
urt appointments; he disturbed London by a rowdy youth;
was reported to have passed on his mistresses to the King;
ended his life in mental and moral decay with a squalid
oman at Bath. He followed the fashions of his age, and the
ost that can be claimed for him is that he should stand, along
th his inseparables Rochester and Sedley, as the prototype
that age. But for all that, there is about such geniality, such
nerosity, and such munificence, a certain coarse lovableness
hich holds an indestructible charm for the English race. It
that which makes Charles the Second a more popular
onarch than William the Third: Herrick a more popular
et than Milton. Last but not least, Charles Sackville is
nnected with that most attractive figure of the English stage—
ell Gwyn.

It is not known precisely in what year he was born, but it
as either 1639, 1640, or 1642, so that he must have been a
ung man somewhere in the neighbourhood of twenty when
harles II came to the throne. He had been educated by a
tor, one Jennings, and sent abroad with him: as Jennings
rote home of him in measured terms surprising in that age
sycophancy, saying "I doubt not he will attain to some per-
ction," he probably held but a low opinion of the abilities of

his pupil. I do not know at what age Lord Buckhurst, as
then was, returned to England, but he must have been qu
young, for in 1660 he becomes Colonel of a regiment of fo
commands 104 men, and receives a yearly allowance of £
from his father, and the references to him in Pepys begin
1661 when he was not more than twenty-one or twenty-tw
He was, says Dr. Johnson with characteristic disapproval a
severity, "eager of the riotous and licentious pleasures whi
young men of high rank, who aspired to be thought wits,
that time imagined themselves entitled to indulge." Many
his pranks have been placed on record. They are neither ve
funny nor very edifying, On one occasion he and his broth
Edward, with three friends, were committed to Newgate f
killing an innocent man in a brawl, and should no doubt ha
been tried for murder, but as those contretemps could be a
ranged with very little difficulty the charge was modified
manslaughter.[1] On another occasion, the full details of whi
are not allowed to remain in the expurgated edition of Pepy
Lord Buckhurst, Sir Charles Sedley, and Sir Thomas Og
got drunk at the Cock Tavern in Bow Street, where they we
out on to a balcony, and Sedley took off all his clothes an
harangued the crowd which collected below: the crowd, in i
dignation, drove them in with stones, and broke the windov
of the house; for this offence all three gentlemen were i
dicted and Sedley was fined £500. On yet another occasio
Buckhurst and Sedley spent the night in prison for brawlir
with the watch, and were delivered only on the King's inte
vention. On yet another, Pepys records that "the King wa
drunk at Saxam with Sedley and Buckhurst, the night that m
Lord Arlington came thither, and would not give him aud
ence, or could not." These and similar exploits recall the mo

[1] The following account is abridged from the *Mercurius Public*
of the day: "Charles Lord Buckhurst; Edward Sackville, his brothe
Sir Henry Belasyse, eldest son of Lord Belasyse; John Belasys
brother of Lord Faulconberg; and Thomas Wentworth, only son
Sir G. Wentworth, whilst in pursuit of thieves near Waltham Cros
mortally wounded an innocent tanner named Hoppy, and . . . we
soon after apprehended on charges of robbery and murder, but th
Grand Jury found a bill for manslaughter only."

lebrated escapade of Rochester as an astrologer, which at
ast had in it a humorous element entirely lacking in the mere
oting of drunken young men like Buckhurst and Sedley. It
not very surprising to learn that although he "inherited not
ly the paternal estate of the Sackvilles but likewise that of
e Cranfields, Earls of Middlesex in right of his mother, yet
his decease his son, then only eighteen years of age, pos-
ssed so slender a fortune that his guardians when they sent
m to travel on the Continent allowed him only eight hundred
ounds a year for his provision," nor that "extenuated by
easures and indulgences, he sank into a premature old age."
fore sinking into this old age, however, he lived through the
ll enjoyment of a splendid youth. It is difficult to imagine
era in English history more favourable to a young man of
s type and fortune than the early years of Charles II, when
e King himself was the ringleader in the outburst of revolt
ainst that iron-grey period of Puritanism through which the
untry had just passed. Dresses became extravagant, silver
nate, speech licentious; the theatres, which had been closed
r over twenty years, reopened, the costumes and scenery
ing now on an elaborate scale never contemplated before;
omen—a daring innovation—appeared in the women's
les; the King and his brother patronized the play-houses
th all the young bloods of the court; coaches clattered
rough the streets of London, yes, even on a Sunday. There
, of course, another side to the picture—the sullen dis-
pproval of the serious-minded, the squalor of a London
ortly to be rotted by plague and terribly purified by fire—
it with this side we have in the present connection no con-
rn. We are in the gay upper stratum of prosperity and
shion, fortunate in the extraordinary vividness of our visual-
ation; we know not only the principal characters, but also
e crowd of "supers" pressing behind them; we know their
omings and goings, their intrigues, their rivalries, their
nusements, the names of their mistresses. We are now at
Whitehall, now at Epsom, now at Tunbridge Wells, now at
ichmond. We are, indeed, very deeply in Pepys' debt.

In this world, therefore, so intimately familiar to any reader

of the great diarist, Lord Buckhurst moves noisily with Roc[h]
ester and Buckingham, Etherege and Sedley, "the first gentl[e]
man," says Horace Walpole, "of the voluptuous court [of]
Charles II." We are told that he refused the King's offers [of]
employment in order to enjoy his pleasures with the great[er]
freedom, or, as he himself wrote with much frankness:

> *May knaves and fools grow rich and great,*
> * And the world think them wise,*
> *While I lie dying at her feet,*
> * And all the world despise.*

> *Let conquering Kings new triumphs raise,*
> * And melt in court delights:*
> *Her eyes can give much brighter days,*
> * Her arms much softer nights.*

This did not prevent him from enrolling as a volunteer i[n]
the Dutch war of 1665, when he was present at a naval battl[e,]
and when the song which he was reported to have written o[n]
the eve of the engagement was brought to London and bandie[d]
from mouth to mouth about the town. Dr. Johnson show[s]
himself sceptical as to this picturesque legend of the origin [of]
the verses. "Seldom is any splendid story wholly true," h[e]
observes; and continues, "I have heard from the Earl [of]
Orrery, that Lord Buckhurst had been a week employed upo[n]
it, and only re-touched, or finished it, on the memorabl[e]
evening." However this may be, both song and story remain[.]
I have told the story, and quote the song:

> *To all you ladies now at land*
> *We men at sea indite;*
> *But first would have you understand*
> *How hard it is to write:*
> *The Muses now, and Neptune too,*
> *We must implore to write to you,*
> *   With a fa, la, la, la, la.*

> *For though the Muses should prove kind*
> * And fill our empty brain,*
> *Yet if rough Neptune rouse the wind*
> * To wave the azure main,*

Our paper, pen and ink, and we,
Roll up and down our ships at sea,
    With a fa, la, la, la, la.

Then if we write not by each post,
    Think not we are unkind;
Nor yet conclude our ships are lost
    By Dutchman or the wind:
Our tears we'll send a speedier way,
The tide shall bring them twice a day,
    With a fa, la, la, la, la.

The King with wonder and surprise
    Will swear the seas grow bold,
Because the tides will higher rise
    Than e'er they did of old:
But let him know it is our tears
Bring floods of grief to Whitehall stairs,[1]
    With a fa, la, la, la, la.

Should foggy Opdam chance to know
    Our sad and dismal story,
The Dutch would scorn so weak a foe
    And quit their fort at Goree;
For what resistance can they find
From men who've left their hearts behind?—
    With a fa, la, la, la, la.

Let wind and weather do its worst,
    Be you to us but kind,
Let Dutchmen vapour, Spaniards curse,
    No sorrow we shall find:
'Tis then no matter how things go,
Or who's our friend, or who's our foe,
    With a fa, la, la, la, la.

To pass our tedious hours away
    We throw a merry main,
Or else at serious ombre play;
    But why should we in vain

[1] This refers to the frequent flooding of Whitehall Palace by an
unusually high tide.

Each other's ruin thus pursue?
We were undone when we left you,
    With a fa, la, la, la, la.

But now our fears tempestuous grow
    And cast our hopes away;
Whilst you, regardless of our woe,
    Sit careless at a play;
Perhaps permit some happier man
To kiss your hand, or flirt your fan,
    With a fa, la, la, la, la.

When any mournful tune you hear
    That dies in every note
As if it sighed with each man's care
    For being so remote,
Think then how often love we've made
To you, when all those tunes were played,
    With a fa, la, la, la, la.

In justice you cannot refuse
    To think of our distress,
When we for hopes of honour lose
    Our certain happiness:
All those designs are but to prove
Ourselves more worthy of your love,
    With a fa, la, la, la, la.

And now we've told you all our loves,
    And likewise all our fears.
In hopes this declaration moves
    Some pity for our tears;
Let's hear of no inconstancy,
We have too much of that at sea—
    With a fa, la, la, la, la.

With this song—which is really quite good of its kind, and
I think, deserves its anthology fame—Pepys says that h
"occasioned much mirth," although at the time of repeating
he was under the impression that it was written by three autho
in collaboration. It seems to have achieved popularity, and wa

to music, also a parody was written of it by Lord Halifax der the title "The New Court: Being an Excellent New Song an old Tune of 'To all you Ladies now at hand' by the Earl Dorset," and of which the following is the opening verse:

> To all you Tories far from Court
>   We Courtiers now in play
> Do write, to tell you how we sport
>   And laugh the hours away.
> The King, the Turks, the Prince, and all
> Attend with us each Feast and Ball.
>   With a fa, etc.

It is shortly after this battle that Nell Gwyn first appears in ord Buckhurst's life. London's two theatres—the Duke's heatre, near Lincoln's Inn Fields, and the King's Theatre, , more familiarly, The Theatre, in Drury Lane—were then e great new resort and amusement, from the King and his other in their boxes down to the rabble in the pit. Until the ign of Charles II the presence of the King in a common ay-house was an unknown thing: such plays or masques as ey had witnessed were always specially performed for them ther in the halls or cock-pits of their palaces, but it now ecame the fashion for not only the King and the Duke of ork, but also for the Queen to patronize the theatres. There ere other innovations. The public was no longer satisfied ith the makeshift scenery of pre-Commonwealth days, which ad too often consisted of a placard hung upon a nail, "*A ood*," or "*A throne-room*," or whatever it might be. Nor were he dresses of the actors as careless as they had formerly been, ut patrons of the stage would give their old clothes, which, if habby, were no doubt still sufficiently magnificent to produce heir effect at a distance. Even a step further in progress was he appearance of women on the stage, "foul and undecent vomen now, and never till now, permitted to appear and act," ays Evelyn, full of indignation, "who, inflaming several young oblemen and gallants, became their misses and to some their vives, witness the Earl of Oxford, Sir R. Howard, Prince Rupert, the Earl of Dorset, and another greater person than

any of them." A theatre of that day must have been a nois[e]
ruffling, ill-lighted place. The ceiling immediately above t[he]
pit was either open to the sky or else inadequately cover[ed]
over, so that in the event of rain the whole of the pit was a[ble]
to surge into the dry parts of the theatre. The ladies in t[he]
audience, especially if the performance happened to be [a]
comedy, sat for the most part in masks. The sallow face of t[he]
King, framed by the heavy curls, leered down over the ed[ge]
of a box. In the body of the theatre lounged the bucks of t[he]
town, exchanging pleasantry and impudence with the orang[e]
girls who were so indispensable a feature.

These orange-girls stood in the pit, crying "Oranges! w[ill]
you have any oranges?" and were under the control of a superi[or]
known as Orange Moll, a famous figure of London theat[re]
life. One may quote, to give some further idea of the relatio[ns]
between the young dandies and the orange-sellers, some of th[e]
stage directions in Shadwell's *True Widow*, in the fourth ac[t]
laid in the Playhouse, "Several young coxcombs fool with th[e]
orange-women," or "He sits down and lolls in the orang[e]
wench's lap," or, "Raps people on the back and twirls the[ir]
hats, and then looks demurely, as if he did not do it." Among[st]
these girls, at the beginning of her career, was Nell Gwyn, [of]
whom Rochester wrote:

> . . . . the basket her fair arm did suit,
> Laden with pippins and Hesperian fruit;
> This first step raised, to the wondering pit she sold
> The lovely fruit smiling with streaks of gold,

and who has come down to us as a figure full of disreputab[le]
charm, witty Nelly, pretty Nelly, Nelly whose foot was leas[t]
of any woman's in England, Nelly who paid the debts of thos[e]
whom she saw being haled off to prison, Nelly the pert, th[e]
apt, the kind-hearted, Nelly who "continued to hang on he[r]
clothes with her usual negligence when she was the King'[s]
mistress, but whatever she did became her." This merr[y]
creature said of herself that she was brought up in a broth[el]
and served strong waters to gentlemen: it is probable that sh[e]
was born in the Coal Yard at Drury Lane (now Goldsmit[h]

reet), and, wherever she may have been brought up, at a
ry early age she joined the orange-girls at the King's
heatre. In due time her looks and her wit attracted attention
d she went on the stage. Pepys, who was evidently much
ken with the "bold merry slut," leaves a particularly
arming record of her one May day:

May 1st. To Westminster, in the way meeting many milk-
aids with their garlands upon their pails, dancing with a
ddler before them; and saw pretty Nelly standing at her
dgings door in Drury Lane in her smock sleeves and bodice,
oking upon one; she seemed a mighty pretty creature.

his being in May (1657), when Nell was sixteen, and had
ready been acting for at least two years, in July of the same
ar the diarist was told, which troubled him, that "my Lord
uckhurst hath got Nell away from the King's House, and
ves her £100 a year, so as she hath sent her parts to the house
d will act no more."

> *None ever had so strange an art*
> *His passion to convey*
> *Into a listening virgin's heart*
> *And steal her soul away*

as sung of Buckhurst. He was then twenty-seven or so, Nell
wyn sixteen, and together they kept "merry house" at
psom. Pepys went down to Epsom one day and heard reports
f their merriments: he pitied Nelly, exclaiming, "Poor girl!"
nd pitied still more her loss to the King's Theatre; but he
oes not expressly state whether he saw the pair or not. In
ny case, the housekeeping at Epsom did not continue for
ery long, for by August she was again acting in London, and
epys had "a great deal of discourse with Orange Moll, who
ells us that Nell is already left by my Lord Buckhurst, and
hat he makes sport of her, and swears she hath had all she
ould get of him." It would appear from this that Buckhurst,
ontrary to what has been said of him, did not sell Nell Gwyn

to the King, for even Pepys, who would surely have be
among the first and best informed, does not mention the Ki
having "sent for Nelly" until January of the following ye
I hope, therefore, that the charges of his having accept
bribes in exchange for Nelly may be exploded. A great ma
things were whispered—that he had been promised the peera
of Middlesex, that he had been given a thousand pounds
year, that he had been sent on "a sleeveless errand" in
France to leave the coast clear for the King, that he refused
give her up until he had been repaid for all the expenses s
had entailed upon him. I do not think that such a Jewish spi
is at all in keeping with the rest of his character as we know
with his generosity and general lavishness, nor does it see
probable that he would so have bargained with a king who
favour he was anxious to retain. By 1669 it is certain that N
was definitely the King's mistress and all connection wi
Buckhurst over. But we find that years afterwards the hou
called Burford House, at Windsor, is granted by Charles
to Charles, Earl of Dorset and Middlesex, W. Chaffinch, Esq
and others, in trust for Ellen Gwyn for life, with remainder
the Earl of Burford, the King's natural son, in tail male
further, among the Knole papers is the original deed of 168
appointing Lord Dorset her trustee and trustee to her son b
Charles II; and, dated 1678, there is an allusion to her forme
lover in one of Nell's infrequent and ill-spelt letters: "M
lord Dorseit apiers worze in thre months, for he drinks ai
with Shadwell and Mr. Haris at the Duke's house all day long.

Nell Gwyn thus passed out of Lord Buckhurst's life, whic
she had so briefly entered, a well-assorted pair, I think, i
every respect—he, idle, spoilt, heavy and magnificent; she
coarse, witty, feminine. There is a portrait of her at Knole
which I suppose was acquired by him, and I once happene
to see a set of spoons in a loan exhibition which were cata
logued as bearing the arms of Sackville with those of Nel
Gwyn. The Sackville shield was correct enough, but whethe
the other quarterings were the arms of Gwyn, or whethe
indeed the orange-girl was entitled to any heraldic device,
am, of course, unable to say.

RICHARD SACKVILLE
3rd Earl of Dorset, 1589–1624

THE SOUTH SIDE AND THE ORANGERY

Geo. P. King

THE GREEN COURT

Country Life

THE SOMERSET HOUSE CONFERENCE OF 1604
Thomas Sackville, 1st Earl of Dorset, sits at the top
right-hand corner, nearest the window

Geo. P. King

LADY ANNE CLIFFORD

THE BROWN GALLERY

Country Life

Geo. P. K

EDWARD SACKVILLE
4th Earl of Dorset, 1589-1652

THE SONS OF EDWARD, 4TH EARL OF DORSET

chard, Lord Brockhurst (left), The Hon. Edward Sackville (right)

THE LEICESTER GALLERY

Geo. P. K.

CHARLES SACKVILLE
6th Earl of Dorset, 1637 (*or* '36)–1706

THE STONE COURT   *Derek Adkins*

THE SPANGLE ROOM

Country Life

KNOLE FROM THE AIR

Aero Pictorial Ltd.

Geo. P.

JOHN FREDERICK SACKVILLE
3rd Duke of Dorset, 1745–1799

Geo. P. King

LADY BETTY GERMAIN
1680–1769

Geo. P. K

THE THREE CHILDREN

George John Frederick Sackville, 4th Duke of Dorset

Lady Mary Sackville   Lady Elizabeth Sackville

THE GREAT STAIRCASE   *Geo. P. King*

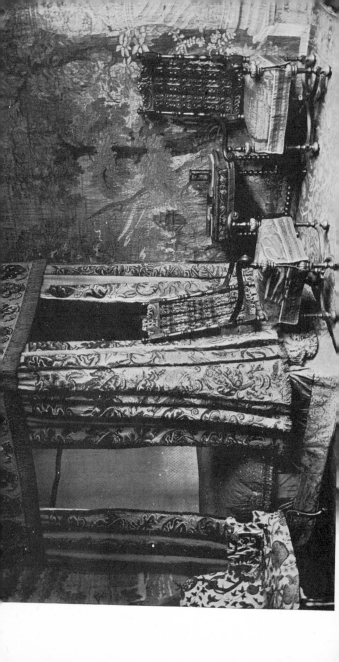

§ iii

Pomp, wealth, and infirmities now began to take the place
brilliant youth and irresponsibility. The frivolous Lord
ckhurst became Earl of Dorset and Middlesex, he suc-
eded to the estates of the Cranfields, he married, he was
ade Lord Chamberlain, he was given the Garter, and he had
fit of apoplexy in the King's bedroom. In order to recover
s health he went abroad; his passport is at Knole, on yellow
rchment, with the King's signature at the top:

Charles the *Second* by the Grace of God, etc., to all admirals,
ce-admirals, captains of our ships at sea, governors,
mmanders, soldiers, mayors, sheriffs, justices of the
ace, bailiffs, constables, customers, controllers, searchers,
d all other our loving subjects whom it may concern,
eeting:

Whereas our right trusty and right well-beloved cousin
HARLES Earl *of* Dorset *and* Middlesex hath desired our
ence to go beyond the seas for recovery of his health, we
e graciously pleased to condescend thereunto, and accord-
gly our will and pleasure is, and we do hereby require, that
u permit and suffer the said Charles Earl of Dorset and
iddlesex with six servants by name Richard Raphael, Robert
nnock, Thomas Bridges, — Solomon, John Carter, and
ristopher Garner, also forty pounds in money, and all bag-
ge, utensils, carriages, and necessaries to the said Earl
longing, freely to embark in any of our ports and from
ence to pass beyond the seas without any let, hindrance, or
olestation whatsoever. And you are likewise to permit the
id Earl and his servants at their return back into this King-
m to pass with like freedom, into the same, affording them
s there may be occasion] all requisite aid and furtherance
well going as returning. And for so doing this shall be your
arrant.
Given at our court at Windsor, the 23rd day of *August*
81, in the three and thirtieth year of our reign.

By his Ma^{ty's} Command,

L. JEN KINS

There is also a letter from one of the servants mentioned the passport, saying that they had had a good passage Dieppe, "except Mr. Raphael, who was kind to ye fishes."

There is another letter, from the Mr. Raphael in questio written home to Robert Pennock from Paris while on the sam journey, saying that his Lordship wants the pond finish against the spring, orders the gardener to manure all the tree and wishes Pennock to obtain a sure-footed nag, as his Lor ship intends for the future only to make use of a saddle-hor between Copt Hall and London to prevent the pain of t gravel, of which infirmity his Lordship has lately been mu troubled.

About this time he married. I have in my hands one of h love-letters, in faded ink; there is no date, no beginning, a no signature: it is superscribed "for the Countess of Fa mouth," and enclosed is a lock of reddish-brown hair—mo dead and poignant token—of surprising length when o considers the heavy wig which was to be worn over it.

I must beg leave that we may be a little earlier than ordina at Hick's hall today, for tomorrow, i may be so miserable not to see you; besides i am in pain till i can clear some doub that have kept me waking all night; something i observed your looks which shewed you had been displeased, at what dare not ask; but till i know i must suffer the torment of un certain guessing; though i am pretty well assured i could n be concerned in it [more than in the trouble it gave you]; bein so perfectly yours, that it will of necessity be counted yo own fault if ever i offend you, since 'tis you alone have th government not only of all my actions but of my very thought to confirm you in the belief of this truth i do from this mome give up to you all my pretences to freedom or any power ove myself, and though you may justly think it below you to b owned the sovereign of so mean a dominion as my heart, i hav yet confidence upon my knees to offer it you; since never an prince could boast of so clear a title, and so absolute powe as you shall ever possess in it.

We know a good deal about Lord Dorset's expenses an finances. We know that on the death of his mother he obtaine

additional income of £1744 14s. 11d. a year from her
tes. We know that thirty-four houses in the Strand were
ted to him, and let as follows:

	£	s.	d.
3 houses at from £6 to £65 each	950	7	1
houses built by him and let at £90 each	270	0	0
Total	£1220	7	1

know that twenty-four tenements east of Somerset House
e granted to him for ninety-nine years at a yearly rent of
10s. 4d.—and that out of them he should have made
768 a year, as witness the list I reproduce, taken from a
nuscript at Knole, but either he or his bailiff must dis-
cefully have neglected his business, for on Lord Dorset's
th many rents were found to be in arrear, one tenant's
rly rent of £30 having accumulated to the sum of £235
6d., or nearly eight years' owing, and another rent of
7 18s. 4d. had accumulated to arrears of £111 19s. 10½d.
servants' accounts, too, were in a state of confusion, and
ne of the wages unpaid up to three years.

Signs	£	s.	d.
The Rising Sun	64	0	0
7 Stars and King's Arms	60	0	0
	60	0	0
	110	0	0
Surgeon's Arms	60	0	0
The Golden Ball	60	0	0
„ „ Key	60	0	0
	60	0	0
Mitre	90	0	0
3 Golden [?]	90	0	0
Black Lion	90	0	0
Golden Fleece	40	0	0
	60	0	0
Golden [?]	48	0	0
Two Cats	60	0	0
	60	0	0
	70	0	0

	£	s.	d.
Hen and Chicken	60	0	0
Spread Eagle, a Bath house	40	0	0
	13	0	0
3 Black Lions	60	0	0
The Angel	70	0	0
	55	0	0
The Dorset Arms Tavern	140	0	0
Swan	33	0	0
	55	0	0
Bull Head Tavern	24	0	0
The Dial	34	0	0
Ship and Bale	34	0	0
The Peacock	8	0	0
	1768	0	0

His total income for the year 1698–99 was £7650 4s. 3½d
the curious accuracy of these sums does not seem to tally w
the confusion to which I have referred—that is to say, abo
£40,000 of modern money. It may be interesting, while
this subject, to show some of the means common among
great nobles for filling their pockets. In 1697, for instance,
read that "My Lord Chamberlain Dorset has sold the keep
ship of Greenwich Park to the Earl of Romney" [James Vern
to Matthew Prior], and in the same year—this is when he w
getting on in years and entirely withdrawing from politics
"Lord Dorset hath resigned his office of Lord Chamberla
to the Earl of Sunderland for the sum of ten thousand pounds
but where was this sum to come from? not out of Lord Sunde
land's pocket; no, but "*which his Majesty pays.*" There w
yet another method by which money might conveniently b
raised: it is well illustrated by Dorset's petition regarding th
dues on tobacco:

To the King's most Ex^t Ma^ty
The Humble Petition of CHARLES Earl *of* Middlesex.
    Humbly Sheweth
        That by the act [for preventing planting of tobacco i
    England and for regulating the Plantation Trade] a

ships that shall return from any of yr Maj^ties foreign
plantations and not return to yr Maj^ties Kingdom of
England, Dominion of Wales or Town of Berwick upon
Tweed, and there pay the customs and duties . . . shall
be confisable and their bonds forfeited. That the *Phenix* of
London, Richard Pidgeon Commander and several other
ships have . . . discharged merchandizes of the growth of
yr Maj^ties Plantations, in yr Kingdom of Ireland, so that
by law they are forfeited as by the said Act produceable
may appear.

May it therefore please yr Sacred Maj^ty to grant yr
Petitioner all forfeitures as well past as to come on
accompt of the said Act, with power to depute such
persons as he shall think fitting, to look upon and take
care that no such abuses shall be in ye future.

[*Knole MSS.* 1671.]

To this petition I should like to add another, representing
the other point of view, that of the unfortunate people who
had the King's soldiers quartered upon them in intolerable
numbers, and were, as it appears, not refunded for the expenses to which they had been put. I add this the more
willingly, as Dorset was commonly reputed the friend of the
poor, and it is said of him that "crowds of poor daily thronged
his gates, expecting thence their bread. The lazy and the sick,
if he accidentally saw them, were removed from the street to
the physician, and not only cured but supplied with what
might enable them to resume their former calling. The
prisoner has often been released by my Lord's paying the
debt, and the condemned been pardoned, through his
intercession with the sovereign."

To the Right Honble CHARLES Earl *of* Dorset *and* Middlesex.

The humble petition of the Innholders and Alehouse
Keepers in the parish of Sevenoaks in the county of
Kent, Humbly Sheweth,

That your said petitioners have every year since ye
coming of his present Majesty had either foot or horse
quartered on them, even much beyond their neighbours
. . . The said innkeepers are willing to serve their King and
Country, but beyond their ability cannot, they therefore

humbly pray that care may be taken for procuring th
arrears due, or at least so prevent more soldiers comi
on them, which they understand are, unless your Hono
will stand in the gap . . .

[*Knole MS.*

Some of the foregoing papers, then, account for his incon
we have also some notes as to his expenses. To his serva
he paid £8 to £10 a year for "ordinary men and maids." F
beef he paid 2s. a stone; for mutton, 3d. a pound; pullets we
6d. each; a goose was 1s. 8d.; a pheasant, 1s.; a hare, 8d.
tongue, 1s.; a partridge, 9d.; a pigeon, 3d.; a turkey, 2s. 6d.
calf's head, 1s. 6d. A bushel of oysters cost him 4s. 6d.; a pe
of damsons, 1s. Wheat cost him 7s. a bushel; salt, 5s. a bush
For 130 walnuts he paid 1s. 6d., and for a dozen candles 5s. 6
—a surprising price. We have also a detailed account of h
cellar. For strong beer he paid 35s. a hogshead, and for sm
beer 10s. a hogshead. From July 1690 to November 1691 h
total wine bill amounted to £598 19s. 4d., an alarming su
when we reflect that he was paying only 5s. 1d. for a gallo
of red port, 6s. 8d. for a gallon of sherry, and 8s. for a gallon
canary. We are given the details entered in the cellar fro
August 1690 to January 1691; they are sufficiently formidabl
425 gallons of red port, 85 gallons of sherry, 72 gallons
canary, 63 gallons of white port, and a quart of hock. On
wonders whether Lord Dorset was "laying down," or wheth
this quantity was adequate only to the six months shown o
the account book.

Lord Dorset seems to have carried large sums of mone
about on his person, for the steward's account book at Knol
shows a regular daily entry of 10s. for loose change to h
Lordship, and when he was set upon by footpads near Tybur
they robbed him not only of his gold George, but also of fort
or fifty pounds. This does not perhaps seem a very enormou
sum for a wealthy man to carry, but it must always be remem
bered that in order to obtain the modern equivalent it i
necessary to multiply by at least five.

Before leaving the Knole papers of this date—and there i

ch that I have regretfully discarded, many letters, for
tance, regarding the election of Lord Buckhurst to the
use of Commons, which throw interesting sidelights upon
methods of electioneering in the early days of Charles II—
hould like to quote one letter of unknown authorship,
ting to the Rye House Plot. The letter is addressed to Lord
rset: it is unsigned and undated, but the date must be
ced, by virtue of internal evidence, in July 1683, by reason
he reference to Captain Walcot who was tried on July 12th
connection with the plot.

The party that went for my Lord Essex found him in his
·den gathering of nut-meg peaches, he was lodged in my
·rd Feversham's lodgings, in Whitehall, and the next day,
ving not made use of the favour of pen and ink, so well as
· Lord Howard hath, he was sent to the Tower.
My Lord Howard runs like a spout, fresh, and fresh he hath
it enough to hang himself, and 1 hundred more, and cried
ough to drown himself, he hath cast his lodgings in
hitehall.
Sir John Burlace was brought before the Council yesterday,
on sending intelligence to my Lord Lovelace that there was
varrant against him. He stayed one night in the messenger's
nds and was this morning bail for my Lord Lovelace, and
th of them dismissed.
The enclosed is an account how far the Grand Jury hath
oceeded, that little note hath the names of some of the
rand Jury.
None were tried this afternoon but Capt. Walcot who was
st by a most clear evidence being at several consults, the
ices all named, his raising of arms, his own letter to the
ng, and one of the consults was at the Vulture, Ludgate
ll, and Sheppard's House, he had very little to say for him-
f, but that the witnesses swore away his life to secure their
vn, he excepted against all Jury men that were of the
utenancy and behaved himself with a great deal of decency
d resolution. They had a declaration ready drawn by
oodenough so soon as ever the King was killed, and particular
en appointed to murder the most considerable persons.
rne by name was to kill this Lord Keeper, and refused it

because it looked like an unneighbourly thing, my Lord pul
off his hat and said Thank you, neighbour.

I find also, dated 1690, this curious vocabulary of thiev
slang scribbled on the back of some particulars relating to
appointment of a new incumbent for Sevenoaks. Unfortunat
half the alphabet is missing:

Autem mort	a marryed woman
Abram	naked
abram-cour	a tatterdemalion
autem	a church
boughar	a cur
bouse	drink
bousing-ken	an ale-house
borde	a shilling
boung	a purse
bing	to goe
bing a wast	to goe away
bube	ye pox
buge	a dog
bleating-cheat	a sheep
billy-cheat	an apron
bite ye peter or Roger	steal ye portmantle
budge	one that steals cloaks
bulk and file	a pickpocket and his mate
cokir	a lyar
cuffin quire	a justice
crampings	bolts and shackles
chats	ye gallows
crackmans	hedges
calle ⎫	
togeman ⎬	a cloak
Joseph ⎭	
couch	to lye asleep
couch a hogshead	to goe to sleep
commission	
mish	a shirt
cackling-cheat	a chicken
cassan	cheese
crash	to kill

crashing-cheat	teeth
cloy	to steal
cut	to speak
cut bien whydds	to speak well
cut quire whydds	to speak evill
confeck	counterfeit
cly ye jerk	to be whipt
dimber	pretty
damber	rascall
drawers	stockings
duds	goods
deusea vile	ye country
dommerer	a madman
darkmans	night or even
dup	to enter
tip me my earnest	give me my part
filch	a staffe
ferme	a hole
fambles	hands
fambles cheats	rings and gloves
fib	to beat
flag	a groat
fogus	tobacco
fencing cully	one that receives stolen goods
glimmer	fire
glaziers	eyes
granna	corne
gentry more	a gallant wench
gun	lip
gage	a pot or pipe
grunting-cheat	a sucking pig
giger	a dore
gybe	a passe
glasier	one that goes in at windows
gilt	a picklock
harmanbeck	a constable
heave a book	to rob a house
half berd	sixpence
heartsease	20 shillings
knapper of knappers	a sheep stealer
lightmans	morning or day
lib	to tumble

libben	an house
lage	water
libedge	a bed
lullabye-cheat	a child
lap	pottage
lucries	all manner of clothes
maunder	to beg
magery prater	an hen
muffling-cheat	a napkin
mumpers	gentile beggars[1]

§ iv

In 1685 Charles II died, and with him departed that devil-may-care existence into which Lord Dorset had fitted so readily and so well. He was no favourite with the new King, for one thing he had addressed verses in this vein to Lady Dorchester, mistress of James II:

> *Tell me, Dorinda, why so gay,*
> *Why such embroidery, fringe, and lace?*
> *Can any dresses find a way*
> *To stop th' approaches of decay,*
> *And mend a ruined face?*
>
> *Wilt thou still sparkle in the box,*
> *Still ogle in the ring?*
> *Canst thou forget thy age and pox?*
> *Can all that shines on shells and rocks*
> *Make thee a fine young thing?*

He appears also at this time to have grown more serious in his outlook, for he disapproved of the new King so strongly as to have taken an active part in the accession of William III to the English throne. He was instrumental, indeed, in arranging the escape of Princess (afterwards Queen) Anne:

That evening [*says Macaulay*] Anne retired to her chamber as usual. At dead of night she rose, and, accompanied by her

---

[1] *See* Appendix I, p. 213.

nd Sarah [Churchill] and two other female attendants,
e down the back stairs in a dressing-gown and slippers.
fugitives gained the open street unchallenged. A hackney
ch was in waiting for them there. Two men guarded the
ble vehicle. One of them was Compton, Bishop of Lon-
, the princess' old tutor; the other was the magnificent
accomplished Dorset, whom the extremity of the public
ger had roused from his luxurious repose. The coach
ve instantly to Aldersgate Street . . . there the princess
sed the night. On the following morning she set out for
ing Forest. In that wild tract [it is amusing to think of
ing as a wild tract]—in that wild tract Dorset possessed a
erable mansion [Copt Hall], the favourite resort, during
ny years, of wits and poets . . .

Macaulay was evidently not in possession of, or else
red (although it is difficult to believe that the incident
ld not have tempted his picturesque and vivid pen), the
ail related by Dorset's grandson, Lord George Sackville,
t

of her Royal Highness' shoes sticking fast in the mud, the
dent threatened to impede her escape; but Lord Dorset,
nediately drawing off his white glove, put it on the Princess'
t, and placed her safely in the carriage.

'hat Lord Dorset had no sympathy with popery is proved
his letter, which is among the Duke of Rutland's papers:

ord Dorset last night [27th January 1688] while at supper
Lady Northampton's, received the following letter with
ss on top:

+

'Twere pity that one of the best of men should be lost
or the worst of causes. Do not sacrifice a life everybody
alues for a religion yourself despise. Make your peace with
our lawful sovereign, or know that after this 27th of
anuary you have not long to live. Take this warning from
friend before repentance is in vain;

it is apparent that he had not lost touch with his old
nds of the Court of Charles II, for we find, in 1688, that

he placed Knole at the disposal of the Queen Dowa
(Catherine of Braganza),

without any consideration of rent, besides the sole use of
park, and if she makes any alterations to have timber out of
woods for that purpose. The Queen Dowager will consi
repairs of the Lord Dorset's house, which will amount
£20,000.

But whether she availed herself of the offer, for however sh
a period, I cannot say.

Lord Dorset was in favour with William III, and continu
to hold his office of Lord Chamberlain until he resigned it
1697. This was the date when he withdrew from all public l
His second wife[1] had died six years before; Dorset hims
was approaching sixty, and the excesses of his youth had lo
since begun to tell. The end of a life which opened with su
gaiety and *éclat* offers a very sordid picture. From his portr
it is easy to see that he has grown heavy and apoplectic:
features are coarsened and swollen; his double chins hang
folds over his vomulinous robes, his ruffles, and his ribbo
He could not hope to enjoy his life at both ends. Those m
have been good days when he got drunk with Sedley, or ke
house with Nelly at Epsom, or exchanged witticisms with
King in the passages at Whitehall, or sat after supper rou
the dining-room table at Knole with Dryden and Killigr
and Rochester; but after running up the account the debt h
to be paid at last. It was all very well for Prior, who owed h
everything, to get gracefully out of a difficulty by saying th
he drivelled better sense than most men could talk: t
remainder of the account is not pretty to contemplate. "A f
years before he died," is the story told by his grandson, Lo
George Sackville, "he married a woman named Roche of ve
obscure connections, who held him in a sort of captivity do
at Bath, where he expired at about sixty-nine." There i
contemporary letter, which says, "My Lord Dorset owns
marriage with one of his acquaintances, one of the Roch

---

[1] Lady Mary Compton. (*See* a pastoral Pindarick, by Aphra Beh
Vol. VI, pp. 350–356. Heinemann, 1915.)

you think anyone will pity him?" "She suffered few per-
ons to approach him during his last illness, or rather, decay,"
Lord George's account continues, "and was supposed to have
averted his weakness of mind to her own objects of personal
acquisition." He was indeed considered to be fallen into a state
of such imbecility as would render it necessary to appoint
guardians, with a view to prevent his injuring the family
estate, but the intention was nevertheless abandoned. You
have no doubt heard, and it is a fact, that with a view of ascer-
taining whether Lord Dorset continued to be of a sane mind,
Prior, whom he had patronized and always regarded with
predilection, was sent down to Bath by the family. Having
obtained access to the Earl, and conversed with him, Prior
made his report in these words, "Lord Dorset is certainly
greatly declined in his understanding, but he *drivels* so much
better sense even now than any other man can *talk*, that you
must not call me into court as a witness to prove him an idiot."
Congreve, appropriating the gist of the remark, observed after
visiting Dorset on his deathbed, "Faith, he slabbers more wit
being than other people do in their best health." Swift also,
who was an intimate friend of Lady Betty Germain and the
Dorsets in the succeeding generation, remarks that Charles
grew dull in his old age. Ann Roche, who guarded so jealously
her ancient and mouldy bird of Paradise, managed to provide
handsomely for herself under his will. He left her not only the
house in Stable Yard, St. James, which was hers before her
marriage, but also lands and messuages in Sussex, two beds
with the furniture thereunto belonging in his house at Knole,
the furniture of two rooms there, all the household linen there,
and £500 to be increased to £20,000 if his son should die
without issue. The marriage only lasted a short time, for in
1705 Lord Dorset died—old, enfeebled, and semi-imbecile.

It is not surprising to learn that he left a number of illegitimate children: we know of at least four for certain, and there
was probably a fifth, a son, as it is difficult to account otherwise for the William Sackville who writes, signing a remarkably ungrammatical letter with a remarkably beautiful
signature, to ask for money, as he has lately "gained the

affection of a young lady," and this, he promises, will be "t
last trouble that ever I shall give your Lordship; it wou
come very seasonable to my present circumstances who h
been harassed and ruined by the fate of war this four years p:
and have done the government good service, and never r
warded as those that deserved it less has." The other four we
daughters. There is a petition at Knole from one of them:

To the Right Hon. CHARLES Earl *of* Dorset *and* Middlese
Lord Chamberlain of Their Majesties' Household, the humb
petition of MARY SACKVILLE:

That it having pleased ye Almighty to lay his afflicting har
on your petitioner's husband and her two small children for
long time together, having nothing to live upon but his ow
hands' labour, which failing him during his sickness all h
family have suffered thereby and been put to great straigh
and having received much of your Honour's charity, is no
. . . [*illegible*] but hopes that your Lordship will consider it
the hand of accident that is hard upon her.

Your petitioner therefore humbly prays that your Honou
will be pleased to bestow something on her this time that sh
may undergo her calamity with a little more cheerfulness an
alacrity.

According to the will of this Mary Sackville, her circun
stances must have improved, for she leaves £1000 "for th
benefit of Katherine Sackville my sister or reputed sister wh
was born of the body of Mrs. Phillipa Waldgrave, deceased
my late mother or reputed mother." This will is dated 1684, s
I should think the Katherine Sackville referred to is probabl
the "K. S." who was buried at Withyham, aged fourteen, i
1690—humble little initials among the Lady Annes and Lad
Elizabeths who surround her. She had been provided for i
Lord Dorset's will also:

To my natural daughter Katherine Sackville, *alias* Walgrave
£1000.

To my natural daughter Mary Sackville, *alias* Walgrave
£200, and £2000 before settled on her.

To my natural daughter An [*sic*] Lee, *alias* Sackville, th
sum of £500.

It thus seems probable that these daughters were the
ildren of two different mothers, Lee and Walgrave, Wald-
ave, Waldegrave, as it was variously spelt. An agreement at
ole, dated 1674, provides for Phillipa Walgrave to receive
terest on £1000 placed in Mr. Guy's hands by Lord Dorset,
e interest on it to be paid to her yearly, and after her death to
ary Sackville until her marriage or until the age of 21, but
Mrs. Walgrave marries, the £1000 is to be paid to her.
other natural daughter, also named Mary, married Lord
rrery, but I do not know who was her mother.

§ v

He had been one of the most notorious libertines of the
ld time which followed the Restoration. He had been the
rror of the city watch, had passed many nights in the round
use, and had at least once occupied a cell in Newgate. His
ssion for Nell Gwyn, who always called him her Charles
e First, had given no small amusement and scandal to the
wn. Yet, in the midst of follies and vices, his courageous
irit, his fine understanding, and his natural goodness of
art, had been conspicuous. Men said that the excesses in
hich he indulged were common between him and the whole
ce of gay young Cavaliers, but that his sympathy with human
ffering and the generosity with which he made reparation
those whom his friends had injured were all his own. His
sociates were astonished by the distinction which the public
ade between him and them. "He may do what he chooses,"
id Wilmot, "he is never in the wrong." The judgment of
e world became still more favourable to Dorset when he
ad been sobered by time and marriage. His graceful manners,
is brilliant conversation, his soft heart, his open hand, were
niversally praised. No day passed, it was said, in which some
istressed family had not reason to bless his name. And yet,
ith all his good nature, such was the keenness of his wit that
coffers whose sarcasm all the town feared stood in craven fear
f the sarcasm of Dorset. All political parties esteemed and
aressed him, but politics were not much to his taste. Had
e been driven by necessity to exert himself, he would pro-
ably have risen to the highest posts in the state; but he was
orn to rank so high and to wealth so ample that many of the

motives which impel men to engage in public affairs we
wanting to him. . . . Like many other men who, with gre
natural abilities, are constitutionally and habitually indoler
he became an intellectual voluptuary, and a master of all tho
pleasing branches of knowledge which can be acquired witho
severe application. He was allowed to be the best judge
painting, of sculpture, of architecture, of acting, that tl
court could show. On questions of polite learning his decisio
were regarded at all the coffee houses as without appeal. Mo
than one clever play which had failed on the first represent
tion was supported by his single authority against the who
clamour of the pit and came forth successful at the secon
trial. . . .

Macaulay thus summarizes his career and character, and
am led quite naturally to the consideration of one aspect of h
life on which I have scarcely touched, and that is his conne
tion with the men of letters of his day. The often-quote
saying, that Butler owed to him that the court tasted h
Hudibras, Wycherley that the town liked his *Plain Dealer*, an
that the Duke of Buckingham deferred the publication of h
Rehearsal until he was sure that Lord Buckhurst would nc
rehearse it upon him again—this saying had much truth in i
It is better, I think, to quote the disinterested opinion c
Macaulay rather than the panegyrics of Prior or Dryden, o
any of the contemporary authors who stood too greatly i
Dorset's debt for complete impartiality:

Such a patron of letters England had never seen [sa)
Macaulay]. His bounty was bestowed with equal judgment an
liberality, and was confined to no sect or faction. Men o
genius, estranged from each other by literary jealousy o
difference of political opinion, joined in acknowledging hi
impartial kindness. Dryden owned that he had been save
from ruin by Dorset's princely generosity. Yet Montague an
Prior, who had keenly satirized Dryden, were introduced b
Dorset into public life; and the best comedy of Dryden'
mortal enemy, Shadwell, was written at Dorset's country seat
The munificent earl might, if such had been his wish, have
been the rival of those of whom he was content to be the
benefactor. For the verses which he occasionally composed,

studied as they are, exhibit the traces of a genius which, assiduously cultivated, would have produced something great. In the small volume of his works may be found songs which have the easy vigour of Suckling, and little satires which sparkle with wit as splendid as those of Butler.

One can, perhaps, scarcely agree with Macaulay in this estimate of Dorset's literary gifts. The songs he wrote are little more than easy specimens of conventional Restoration verse, and, for my part, I fail to find in them, with the exception of "To all you ladies now at land," any merit which was not shared by all the numerous song-writers of the day. It certainly cannot be claimed for him that he had any of the vigour, originality, or true poetic impulse of his great-great-grandfather, the old Lord Treasurer, and although it may be argued that the age of Elizabeth and the age of the Restoration differed totally in poetic conception and spontaneity I still do not admit that Dorset possessed those qualities which might have made up in one direction for those which were lacking in another. I have already quoted his sea-song, unquestionably the best thing he ever wrote, and, to give point to my argument, will quote two further songs, which may stand as typical examples, the first of his graceful but entirely artificial talent, the second of his satire which caused Rochester to say of him:

> For pointed satire I would Buckhurst choose,
> The best good man with the worst natured muse.

SONG

> Phyllis, for shame, let us improve
>   A thousand different ways
> Those few short moments snatched by love
>   From many tedious days.
>
> If you want courage to despise
>   The censure of the grave,
> Though Love's a tyrant in your eyes,
>   Your heart is but a slave.

My love is full of noble pride
  Nor can it e'er submit
To let that fop, Discretion, ride
  In triumph over it.

False friends I have, as well as you,
  Who daily counsel me
Fame and ambition to pursue
  And leave off loving thee.

But when the least regard I show
  To fools who thus advise,
May I be dull enough to grow
  Most miserably wise.

To CATHERINE SEDLEY [married Sir David Colyear]

Proud with the spoils of royal cully,
  With false pretence to wit and parts,
She swaggers like a battered bully
  To try the tempers of men's hearts.

Though she appear as glittering fine
  As gems, and jets, and paints can make her,
She ne'er can win a breast like mine:
  The Devil and Sir David take her.

The fugitive character of his own verses does not, however, in any way detract from his splendour as a patron. It is well known that Matthew Prior as a boy was found by him reading Horace in a tavern in Westminster, when, struck by his intelligence, Dorset sent the boy at his own expense to school until his election as King's Scholar. Prior in after years did not forget this kindness. His poems are dedicated to the son of his earliest patron, and there are, as students of Prior will remember, several amongst them especially written to members of Dorset's family, notably the "Lines to Lord Buckhurst [Dorset's son] when playing with a cat." The many letters from Prior to Lord Dorset, now in Lord Bath's possession, testify to the endurance of their friendship: one of these letters ends with a poem, which I quote, as I am under the impression that it is not included in any edition of Prior's works:

Spare Dorset's sacred life, discerning Fate,
And Death shall march through camps and courts in state,
Emptying his quiver on the vulgar great:
Round Dorset's board let Peace and Plenty dance,
Far off let Famine her sad reign advance,
And War walk deep in blood through conquered France.
Apollo thus began the mystic strain,
The Muses' sons all bowed and said Amen.

It is perhaps less commonly known that Dryden also owed, another way, much to Dorset. The account is thus given by Macaulay:

Dorset became Lord Chamberlain, and employed his influence and patronage annexed to his functions, as he had long employed his private means, in encouraging genius and alleviating misfortune. One of the first acts which he was under the necessity of performing must have been painful to a man of so generous a nature, and of so keen a relish for whatever was excellent in arts and letters. Dryden could no longer remain Poet Laureate. The public would not have borne to see any papist among the servants of their Majesties; and Dryden was not only a papist, but an apostate. He had, moreover, aggravated the guilt of his apostasy by calumniating and ridiculing the Church which he had deserted. He had, it is facetiously said, treated her as the pagan persecutors of old treated her children. He had dressed her up in the skin of a wild beast, and then baited her for the public amusement. He was removed; but he received from the private bounty of the magnificent Chamberlain a pension equal to the salary which had been withdrawn.

Dryden, apparently, despite this generosity, continued to lament his ill-fortune, and his contemporary Blackmore, in a poem called *Prince Arthur*, satirizes him in the character of *Laurus* for his assiduity at Dorset's doors—Dorset being the *Zakil* of the poem, Sackville in transparent disguise:

The poets' nation did obsequious wait
For the kind dole divided at his gate.
Laurus among the meagre crowd appeared,
An old, revolted, unbelieving bard,
Who thronged, and shoved, and pressed, and would be heard.

Sakil's high roof, the Muses' palace, rung
With endless cries, and endless songs he sung.
To bless good Sakil Laurus would be first;
But Sakil's prince and Sakil's God he cursed.
Sakil without distinction threw his bread,
Despised the flatterer, but the poet fed.

It is true that in his *Essay on Satire*, which, like his *Es*
on Dramatic Poetry, is dedicated in terms of the most outra
ous flattery to Dorset, Dryden makes full acknowledgem
of the obligation:

I must ever acknowledge, to the honour of your Lordship a
the eternal memory of your charity, that, since this revoluti
wherein I have patiently suffered the ruin of my small fortu
and the loss of that poor subsistence which I had from t
kings, whom I had served more faithfully than profitably
myself; then your Lordship was pleased, out of no otl
motive but your own nobleness, without any desert of mi
or the least solicitation from me, to make me a most bounti
present, which at that time, when I was most in want of
came most seasonably and unexpectedly to my relief.

But I think there may be detected, even in this acknowled
ment, the note of whining to which Macaulay, in the contin
ation of the passage I have quoted, draws attention. It is al
related that Dryden, when dining with Dorset, found a hundre
pound note hidden under his plate. In a letter preserved
Knole, in Dryden's beautiful handwriting, he makes furth
acknowledgement, after proffering a petition on behalf o
friend who wished to obtain rooms in Somerset House:

. . . if I had confidence enough, my Lord, I would presun
to mind you of a favour which your Lordship formerly ga
me some hopes of from the Queen; but if it be not proper
convenient for you to ask, I dare give your Lordship no furth
trouble in it, being on so many other accounts already yo
Lordship's most obliged obedient servant,   JOHN DRYDE

We know that Dryden was a constant visitor at Knole; v
have even an anecdote of one of his visits. It is related th
someone proposed that each member of the party should wri
an impromptu, and that Dryden, when the allotted time h

ired, should judge between them. Silence ensued while
h guest wrote busily, or laboriously, upon the sheet of
er provided: Dorset scribbled a couple of lines and threw
own on the table. At the end of the time the umpire rose,
said that after careful consideration he awarded the prize
heir host; he would read out what his Lordship had written;
was: "I promise to pay Mr. John Dryden or order five
ndred pounds on demand. DORSET."

t would be interesting to know who were the other members
he party; perhaps Tom Durfey, perhaps Lady Dorset, who
escribed as "jeune, belle, riche, et sage," perhaps Rochester,
ose portrait hangs in the Poets' Parlour—and I imagine the
ets' Parlour to have been the scene of this little incident, "a
umber of parts and players," said Horace Walpole, "which is
per enough in that house"—a portrait of a young man in a
vy wig, labelled "died repentant after a profligate life," as
not understanding the long words, used to gabble off to
angers along with other piteous little shibboleths when
owing the house. Certainly Shadwell was not there, for he
l Dryden were at mortal enmity; Shadwell, his successor
the Laureateship, another friend and protégé of Dorset's,
cribed by Dryden as being

> Round as a globe, and liquored every chink,
> Goodly and great, he sails behind his link.
> For all this bulk there's nothing lost in Og,
> For every inch that is not fool is rogue,

l who writes of Dorset that he was received by him as a
mber of his family, and furthermore, rather plaintively, in
etter at Knole, beseeching Lord Dorset's intervention, as
ey have put Durfey's play before ours, and this day a play
Dryden's is read to them and that is to be acted before ours
."

Tom Durfey, whose portrait is upstairs in Lady Betty's
m, painted in profile, with surely the most formidable of
hooked noses, was almost a pensioner at Knole, having his
n rooms over the dairy, and is guilty of these execrable
ses in praise of his second home:

THE GLORY OF KNOLE

Knole most famous in Kent still appears,
Where mansions surveyed for a thousand long years,
In whose domes mighty monarchs might dwell,
Where five hundred rooms are, as Boswell[1] can tell!

I do not think that Durfey can have been very grea
esteemed by his patron, nor yet on very intimate terms w
him, but kept rather, contemptuously, as permanent rhymes
to Dorset's little court, for another picture, small, obscu
but entertainingly intimate, shows him in humble compa
in the Steward's Room with Lowry, the Steward; Geor
Allan, a clothier; Mother Moss, whoever she may have bee
Maximilian Buck, the chaplain; and one Jack Randall. H
name is certainly not one of the most illustrious among t
many poets and writers represented on the walls of the Poe
Parlour—Edmund Waller, Matthew Prior, Thomas Flattm;
John Dryden, William Congreve, William Wycherley, Thom
Otway, Thomas Hobbes, John Locke, Samuel Butler, Abr
ham Cowley, Nicholas Rowe, William Cartwright, Sir Kenel
Digby, Alexander Pope. And with this last name I come to t
final tribute paid to the splendid Dorset—Pope's epita
upon his monument in the Sackville chapel at Withyham:

> *Dorset, the grace of courts, the Muses' pride,*
> *Patron of arts, and judge of nature, died.*
> *The scourge of pride, though sanctified or great,*
> *Of fops in learning, and of knaves in state:*
> *Yet soft his nature, though severe his gay,*
> *His anger moral, and his wisdom hay.*
> *Blest satirist! who touched the mean so true,*
> *As showed vice had his hate and pity too.*
> *Blest courtier! who could King and country please,*
> *Yet sacred kept his friendships and his ease.*
> *Blest peer! his great forefather's every grace*
> *Reflected and reflecting in his race,*
> *Where other Buckhursts, other Dorsets shine,*
> *And patriots still, or poets, deck the line.*

[1] The butler, not the biographer

LIONEL SACKVILLE
7th Earl *and* 1st
Duke *of* Dorset

§ i

ᴇ FIRST Duke of Dorset remains to me, in spite of much
ding, an indistinct figure. I do not know whether the
lt is mine or his. Perhaps he was a man of little personality;
tainly he was lacking in the charm of his scapegrace father
of his frivolous grandson, the third duke. And yet he is a
sonage of some solidity: weighty, Georgian solidity. The
thets chosen by his contemporaries to describe him are
concordant enough, "a man of dignity, caution, and
usibility," "worthy, honest, good-natured," "he preserved
he last the good breeding, decency of manner, and dignity
xterior deportment of Queen Anne's time, never departing
n his style of gravity and ceremony," "a large-grown, full
son," and finally—the words come almost with the shock
peing precisely what we were waiting for—"in spite of the
atest dignity in his appearance, he was in private the greatest
er of low humour and buffoonery." He was fitted, if I piece
ether rightly my scraps of evidence, to lead the life of a
ntry gentleman, performing his duty towards his county,
ertaining his friends, enjoying with them after dinner the
humour to which he inclined, rolling out his laughter in
Poets' Parlour, slapping his great thighs, and rejoining his
e afterwards in the spirit of affectionate domesticity which
uced him to begin his letters to her "dear, dear, dear girl,"
"my dear, dear Colly." He lived, says one account of him,
er detailing his amiable qualities as a kind husband and
ier, "in great hospitality all his life, and he was so respected
t when at Knole on Sundays the front of the house was so

crowded with horsemen and carriages as to give it rather
appearance of a princely levee than the residence of a pri
nobleman." It was his misfortune that he was not allowe
remain leading this kind of life so much to his taste: '
poor Duke of Dorset," said Lord Shelburne, "was made
his son to commence politician at sixty." The local off
which he held were well suited to his disposition and abilit
the titles of *Custos Rotulorum, Lord Lieutenant of Kent, C
stable of Dover Castle,* and *Lord Warden of the Cinque Port*
admirably upon his rather provincial dignity. He co
discharge these offices while surrounding himself with frie
and keeping open house at Knole. He was surely happ
Knole, with the duchess and the duchess' friend Lady B
Germain installed in her two little rooms in a corner of
house, and the correspondence with Dean Swift, and
echoes of the Restoration reaching him in the shape of ded
tions from Prior and Pope, who had been his father's frie
He must have been happy superintending the building of
"ruins" in the park, in ordering the removal of the clock f
the roof of the Great Hall to a safer place over Bourch
oriel, in putting up the balustrade in the Stone Court
adding to the picture-gallery his own full-length Kne
painted in Garter robes—a dignified and ponderous addi
—in continuing his father's kindly and contemptuous patr
age of Durfey, in entertaining the Prince of Wales, in recei
the present of a pair of elk-antlers measuring 7 foot from
to tip, in playing at cards with his wife and Lady Betty
watching the bull-baiting in the park, in inspiring the foll
ing tribute on the occasion of his birthday:

> *Accept, with unambitious views,*
> *The tribute of a female muse;*
> *Free from all flattery and art,*
> *She only boasts an honest heart;*
> *An heart that truly feels your worth,*
> *And hails the day that gave you birth;*
> *Of younger men let others boast,*
> *Since Dorset is my constant toast;*

Nor need the gayer world be told
That Dorset never can grow old;

And with unerring truth agree,
There's none so young, so blithe as he,
With sprightly wit his jokes abound,
Well-bred, he deals good-humour round;
The maid forgets her fav'rite swain,
When Dorset speaks, he fights in vain;
The lover too, do all he can,
Strives, but in vain, to hate the man.
With this kind wish I end my lays,
Be ever young with length of days.

r such appreciation of his Christmas hospitality as this:

Our liquor at all times to nature gives fire,
Infuses new blood, and new thoughts can inspire.
Your wife, she may scold, undaunted you'll sing,
For he that is drunk is as great as a King.

In the field, if all night you lie under a willow,
The soft easy snow shall be your down pillow.
There's nothing can hurt you without or within
When you've beef in your belly and Punch in your skin

It is true that certain discordant notes troubled from time
o time this Georgian harmony. The house-steward killed
he black page in the passage; and the duke's sons themselves
vere unsatisfactory; even the favourite son, Lord George, who
vas the apple of his father's eye, fell into disgrace and was
ourt-martialled on a charge of disobedience and cowardice.
"I always told you," said Lord John on hearing of this, "that
George was no better than myself." This affair of the battle
f Minden must have been a heavy blow to the duke, but
lthough Lord George was not exonerated he retained all his
ather's doting affection. Still, the mud had been slung at him
nd not a little had stuck. The two other sons were a source of
orrow: Lord John, after devoting his youth to cricket, went
ff his head; and Lord Middlesex, the eldest of the three, was

an altogether deplorable character, prompting these verse
based upon an old saying about the family:

> Folly and sense in Dorset's race
>   Alternately do run,
> As Carey one day told his Grace
>   Praising his eldest son.
>
> But Carey must allow for once
>   Exception to this rule,
> For Middlesex is but a dunce,
>   Though Dorset be a fool.

I quote the verses as they stand, though "dunce" seem
scarcely the right description to apply to Lord Middlesex, th
dissolute and extravagant man of fashion, who squandere
large sums of money upon producing operas, that "prou
disgusted, melancholy, solitary man," whose conduct savoure
so strongly of madness. Certain family characteristics appeare
in him which had skipped his father, and his father and h
consequently and not unnaturally, were not on very goo
terms. The duke, indeed, did not know what to make of h
eldest son and heir. "Upon my word, Mr. Carey," he sai
when Mr. Carey asked him loudly at the play whether Lor
Middlesex was to undertake the opera again next season. "
have not considered what answer to make to such a question.
Both Lord Middlesex and Lord John being so unsatisfactor
Lord George was, and remained, his father's favourite. Lor
George, in an even greater degree than his father, is an incon
gruity among the Sackvilles, a departure from type. In spit
of all his mistakes, his misjudgments, and his misfortunes, h
was a man of greater ability than most of them, of greate
energy than the common run of his indolent and pleasure
loving race, of a further-reaching ambition. He did not begi
life as the eldest son, coming in due course to be the head o
the family, and languidly accepting the civil or diplomati
posts which were pressed upon him; such career as he ha
he made for himself. Unlike his predecessors or their descen
dants, he was neither an ambassador, a poet, nor a patron of ar

letters—"I have not," he wrote, "genius sufficient for works *mere imagination*"—but first a soldier and then a statesman, h disastrously. It is not my intention to go into the details his public career; my ignorance is too great of the tangle of orgian politics; nor am I qualified to discuss whether he l or did not disobey his orders at Minden, whether he was was not largely responsible for the loss of America, whether did or did not write the *Letters of Junius*; such questions treated in histories of the period. Nor can I deal with the ormous numbers of letters on political subjects written both and to Lord George: I have looked into them more than ce, and have come away merely bewildered by the cross-eads of home politics, by the names of remembered or gotten statesmen, by the fall and reconstruction of Minis-es, by the crises of Whigs and Tories. So I judge it best to ve Lord George alone, "hot, haughty, ambitious, and stinate, a sort of melancholy in his look which runs through the Sackville family," and to seek neither to blacken nor to itewash his character. I scarcely regard him as one of the ckvilles, perhaps because he broke away from the family ditions into unfamiliar paths, perhaps also because he ned his own peerage, inherited from Lady Betty a large use of his own, and led an existence separate from Knole. ving at Knole among its portraits and its legends which ew into the very texture of one's life, it was, I suppose, evitable that one should grow up with pre-conceived affec-ns or indifferences, and for some reason Lord George never akened my interest or my sense of relationship. He was a blic character, not a relation.

§ ii

The early impressions of the first duke, who grew to be so mpous, stout, and good-natured, and whose three sons ve him in their several ways so much anxiety, are not attractive. There is a picture of him as a little slim boy, with s sister and their pet fawn; and there is Lord George's own ecdote of his father's childhood:

My father, having lost his own mother, was brought chiefly by the Dowager Countess of Northampton, his gra mother. She being particularly acceptable to Queen Ma that Princess commanded her always to bring her little gra son, Lord Buckhurst, to Kensington Palace, though at t time hardly four years of age, and he was allowed to am himself with a child's cart in the gallery. King William, almost all Dutchmen, never failed to attend the tea-ta every evening. It happened that her Majesty having afternoon by his desire made tea, and waiting for the Kir arrival, who was engaged on business in his cabinet at other extremity of the gallery, the boy, hearing the Que express her impatience at the delay, ran away to the clos dragging after him the cart. When he arrived at the door, knocked, and the King asking "Who is there?" "Lord Bucl answered he. "And what does Lord Buck want with me replied his Majesty. "You must come to tea directly," said "the Queen is waiting for you." King William immediat laid down his pen and opened the door. Then taking the ch in his arms, he placed Lord Buckhurst in the cart, and seizi the pole drew them both along the gallery to the room which were seated the Queen, Lady Northampton, and t company. But no sooner had he entered the apartments, tha exhausted with the effort, which had forced the blood up his lungs, and being constitutionally asthmatic, he thre himself into a chair, and for some minutes was incapable uttering a word, breathing with the utmost difficulty. T Countess of Northampton, shocked at the consequences her grandson's indiscretion, would have punished him, b the King intervened on his behalf.

When a young man he went on the inevitable Grand Tou This journey, it is fair to assume, which was taken at t instigation of his mother's relations, was designed to keep hi away from the influence of his enfeebled father and of h step-mother, Ann Roche, quite as much as for the benefit his education. His father was very angry at this withdraw of his son from his authority, and wrote to him:

i hear my Lady Northampton has ordered you not to obe me; if you take any notice of what she says i have enough

y power to make you suffer for it beyond what she will make
u amends for. But i cannot imagine you to be such a fool
to be governed by the passion and folly of anybody.

Your affectionate father,

DORSET.

i expect you will come away by the next yocht.

The next yacht, however, came away without Lord Buck-
urst, and the young man did not return to England until
ter his father's death. Shortly after his succession and
turn he married Elizabeth Colyear, his "dear, dear Colly,"
d was appointed Lord Warden of the Cinque Ports at a
lary of £160 a year, and Lieutenant of Dover Castle at £50.
his is the menu and cost of the dinner given by the youthful
ord Warden at Dover Castle on the 16th August, 1709 on his
eing appointed by Queen Anne:

	£	s.	d.
5 Soups	3	0	0
12 dishes of fish	10	16	0
1 Westphalia Ham and five fowls	1	6	0
8 dishes of pullets and oysters, with bacon	4	16	0
10 Almond Puddings	3	0	0
12 haunches of venison, roast	1	16	0
6 dishes of roast pigs	2	2	0
3 dishes of roast geese	1	4	0
12 Venison pasties	6	0	0
12 white Fragacies with Peetets	7	4	0
8 dishes of "ragged" veal	4	16	0

Second Course

14 dishes of ducks, turkeys, and pigeons	8	0	0
15 codlin tarts, creamed	4	10	0
12 dishes of roast lobster	4	16	0
12 dishes of umble pies	4	4	0
10 dishes of fried fish	5	0	0
8 dishes of Chickens and rabbits	4	0	0

Ryders

	£	s.	d.
5 dishes of dried sweetmeats	17	10	0
12 dishes of jelly	4	16	0
6 dishes of Selebub cream	2	8	0

	£	s.
13 dishes of fruit	10	0
8 dishes of Almond Pies gilt	4	16
12 dishes of Custard Florentines	3	12
8 dishes of lobster	3	4
120 Intermediate plates of sorts	9	0

Side-Table

A large chine of beef stuck with flags and banners	5	10
1 loaf of double refined sugar	0	4
Oil and vinegar	0	3
Outcharges and expenses of pewter, carriage, bread, wharfage, turnspits, glasses, mugs, for ten men, horses, use of bakehouse, cooks, coach hire	76	16

This was an office he held intermittently for many yea
and on one occasion, England being then at war with Spai
two hundred and fifty butts, eight hogsheads, and fifty quart
casks of Spanish mountain wine, and one hundred jars
Raisins of the Sun, being washed up at Deal and Sandwic
were adjudged to him as the Lord Warden's perquisite
of flotsam and jetsam.

In 1714 died Queen Anne, and Lord Dorset, with other
was sent to Hanover to announce to George his accession
the English throne. He returned from Hanover with the ne
King, and drove with him in his coach from Greenwich
London. On the way George related that thirty-three yea
earlier he had travelled to England as a suitor for the hand
Queen Anne: returning to Gravesend after the failure of h
mission, he rode a common post-horse, which gave him a fal
so that he arrived at Gravesend covered with mud. The Kir
amused himself in the coach with looking out for the pla
where this misfortune had come upon him, and pointed
out to Lord Dorset, who no doubt joined politely in th
laughter.

Thus began that curious reign of a King who did not kno
the language of his adopted country, who spent as much tim
in his Hanoverian as in his English estates, and infinitel
preferred them, who surrounded himself with Germa

urtiers and mistresses, and who locked up his wife for two-
d-thirty years as a punishment for her infidelity. The
lemnity of Lord Dorset cannot have been out of place in
ch a court. Honours now crowded rapidly upon him,
hough at one moment he was temporarily deprived of all
s offices for taking part in political intrigues. He was made a
night of the Garter, six years later he was made a duke, he
as given the office of Lord Steward, and finally he entered
on the first lap of his unfortunate career as Lord Lieutenant
Ireland. Before this, however, he was for the second time
lled upon to be the bearer of news of accession to a King of
gland. I give the account in Lord George's words:

When the intelligence of his [George I's] decease, which
ok place near Osnabrugh, in the end of July 1727, arrived
London, the Cabinet having immediately met, thought
oper to dispatch the Duke of Dorset with the news to the
rince of Wales. He then resided at Kew, in a state of great
ienation from the King, the two Courts maintaining no
mmunication. Some little time being indispensable to enable
y father to appear in a suitable manner before the new
onarch, he sent forward the Duchess his wife, in order to
nounce the event. She arrived at Kew just as the Prince,
cording to his invariable custom, having undressed himself
ter dinner, had laid down in bed. The Duchess demanding
ermission to see him immediately, on business of the
reatest importance, the servants acquainted the Princess of
Vales with her arrival; and the Duchess, without a moment's
esitation, informed her Royal Highness, that George the
irst lay dead at Osnabrugh, that the Cabinet had ordered
er husband to be the bearer of the intelligence to his suc-
essor, and that the Duke would follow her in a short time.
he added that not a moment should be lost in communicating
) great an event to the Prince, as the Ministers wished him
) come up to London that same evening, in order to summon
Privy Council, to issue a proclamation, and take other
equisite measures, at the commencement of a new reign.
To the propriety of all these steps the Princess assented;
ut at the same time informed the Duchess, that she could not
enture to enter her husband's room, as he had only just taken
ff his clothes and composed himself to sleep. "Besides,"

added she, "the Prince will not give credit to the intelligen
but will exclaim that it is a fabrication, designed for the pu
pose of exposing him." The Duchess continued nevertheles
to remonstrate with her Royal Highness, on the injurious co
sequences of losing time, and adding that the Duke of Dors
would expect to find the Prince not only apprised of it, b
ready to accompany him to London. The Princess of Wa
took off her shoes, opened the chamber door softly, and a
vanced up to the bedside, while my mother remained at th
threshold, till she should be allowed to enter the apartme
As soon as the Princess came near the bed, a voice from und
the clothes cried out in German, *Was ist das?* "I am come, si
answered she, "to announce to you the death of the Kin
which has taken place in Germany." "That is one damn
trick," returned the Prince. "I do not believe one word of it
"Sir," said the Princess, "it is most certain. The Duchess
Dorset has just brought the intelligence, and the Duke will
here immediately. The Ministers hope that you will repair
town this very evening, as your presence there is indispe
sable." Her Royal Highness then threw herself on her knee
to kiss the new King's hand; and beckoning to the Duchess
Dorset to advance, she came in likewise, knelt down, an
assured him of the indisputable truth of his father's deceas
Convinced at length of the fact, he consented to get up an
dress himself. The Duke of Dorset arriving in his coach an
six, almost immediately afterwards, George the Secon
quitted Kew the same evening for London.

George the Second, as Prince of Wales, had been on term
of personal friendship with the duke. He had stayed at Knol
when half an ox, four sheep, and a calf were provided, beside
the following items for his visit:

	£	s.
Butcher	17	0
Bread and flour	4	0
Fowls, butter and eggs	14	15
Poulterer	11	14
Fishmonger	9	4
Confectioner	25	10
Wine	66	0
Beer	35	0

	£	s.	d.
Master-cook's bill	20	9	0
To the cooks	37	12	6
The pewterer	3	12	4
The carrier	9	0	0
Lord Lumley's Grenadiers	3	4	6
	£257	1	4

The duke's first essay in Ireland was not unsuccessful: he ᵗt affairs alone as far as he possibly could and was tolerably ₚpular. It was only the second time, twenty years later, that ₑ and Lord George incurred so much dislike. Into the political ₐsons for this I have already said that I will not, because I ₙnot, enter; I will only quote from a curious lampoon, ₑserved in the British Museum, which was written to cele-ₐte the duke's departure in 1754:

Ringing of the Bell
or
A *Hue* & *Cry* after *Raymond* the *Fox*

By ROGER SPY, Esq.

The bells are ringing, Hark! how they merrily toll. What is ₑ cause of their joy? Or why this cheerful tintinnation? ₕey seem animated, and their rejoicing seems sensible, so ₓpressive of triumph and hilarity are their peals, treble, bass ₙd tenor make excellent harmony, and strike the very heart; ₑ ringers themselves pull with pleasure—what is it they toll ₚrth, or what may the bells be supposed to say?

Interpreter
I'll tell you what they say . . .

St. Patrick's
He was full of Pa-pa tricks,
Says the bell of St. Patrick's.

St. Mary
I wonder how dare he,
Says the bell of St. Mary.

St. Bride
Our acts he belied,
Says the bell of St. Bride.

St. Ann
He played Cat-in-Pan,
Says the bell of St. Ann.

St. Andrew
Bad swash as e'er man drew,
Says the bell of St. Andrew.

St. Peter
No vinegar sweeter,
Says the bell of St. Peter.

St. Owen
In mischief full knowing,
Says the bell of St. Owen.

St. Thomas
The Lord keep him from us,
Says the bell of St. Thomas.

St. Nicholas Without
He put good men out,
Says St. Nicholas Without.

St. Nicholas Within
He put bad men in,
Says St. Nicholas Within.

Castle Bell
You're a very bad parcel,
Says the bell of the Castle,

and so on, in the same vein.

His patronage of the actress Peg Woffington sets him in
more personal and amiable light. I have no evidence to prov
whether he was following in the steps of his father; I onl
know that Peg Woffington's portrait, like that of Nell Gwy

of the Baccelli, is at Knole; that an old play-bill of hers
found behind the panelling in the Great Hall; that the
e gave her a command performance at Dublin; and, finally,
t the following facetious petition—was it written by one
he duke's disrespectful sons?—is among the Knole papers:

his Grace LIONEL Duke *of* DORSET, Lord Lieu[t] *of* Ireland.
The humble Memorial of MARGARET WOFFINGTON, *Spinster*.
st humbly sheweth

That your Memorialist is a woman of great merit and small
tune, and would be proud of an opportunity of shewing
zeal for his Majesty's service by her ready acceptance
faithful discharge of any employment he shall graciously
ase to bestow upon her.

That her friends have been at great expense and trouble in
curing and perusing the list of the several places on this
ablishment, and find her extremely well qualified to dis-
rge the Office of Housekeeper to his Majesty's Castle as it
h not require much greater ability than the Rolls or the
ancellorship of the Exchequer.

That your Memorialist is a true friend to the present Con-
ution in opposition to all Mock Patriots and drinks the
ownlow Majority and the Minority for the Moneybill every
y devoutly.

That she has already by the assistance of whisky made two
siderable Proselytes Patrick O'Donoghoe and Thady Foley
r Chairman tho' one of them had been closeted by Col.
kes and the other taken by the hand by Sir Rich[d] Cox,
d verily believes if the same means were employed, the
position would soon lose its principal supporters.

That your Memorialist can produce two of the greatest
emical Writers of the present age in support of her char-
er. 1st. Peter Willson who has abused her more than once
his *Universal Advertiser*—an honour which he is never
own to confer on any but persons of the first ranks and
aracter. 2[dly] Geo. Faulkner, in whose impartial Journal are
ntained a Score of Poems, One Dozen of Sonnets, Six
ters from some of the best Critics, if you will take their own
rds for it, four Epigrams, besides occasional paragraphs,
composed in her praise, and which are at least as well
itten as they are printed.

That your Memorialist is little versed in the Housekeep
Arithmetic, having never been instructed in the doctrine
Items, Dittos, Sums Total and Balances, which circumsta
it is conceived, will turn out greatly to the advantage of
Government.

That her personal attachment to your Grace is so
known, that odd reports have been raised in relation to so
intimacies that have past between two persons that shall
nameless, and which she defies her adversaries to prove.

Wherefore she humbly hopes that Your Grace will take
premises into your serious consideration, and oblige the pres
Incumbent to resign the said office, your Memorialist pay
her the full value thereof, or if she continues obstinate as
women are apt to do, and refuses to sell, that the revers
may be granted to your Petitioner, and the rather as she c
ceives, if it be not done under your Grace's administrati
there may be some reason to fear it will never be done at all

MARGARET WOFFINGT

Mem: She is ready and willing to act as first Chamberm
to your Grace, to warm your bed and tuck you in, which, as
is advised and verily believes, the present Housekeeper is
no manner qualified to do.

§ iii

I have already mentioned Lady Betty Germain, w
during the lifetime of the first duke and duchess, lived alm
entirely at Knole and had three rooms—her bedroom,
sitting-room, and her china closet—set aside for her exclus
use. This little prim lady, to whom the three little rooms m
have provided so apposite a frame, occupied her time
writing letters, in stitching at crewel work with bright
coloured wools, in making pot-pourri to fill the bowls on
window ledges, and in telling anecdotes of Queen Anne, wh
lady-in-waiting she had once been, since to her, no doubt,
common with all human nature, the days which were the p
were preferable to the days which were the present. She w
primarily, the friend of the Duchess of Dorset, and for o
a woman was installed in the house whose coiffure and pet
coats the wind of scandal was unable to ruffle. They compos

e, the duchess, the duke, and Lord George, a harmonious artette, whose correspondence survives, voluminous and timate, pricked into sharper highlights here and there by e pen of Swift. "As to my duchess," writes Lady Betty, "she so reserved that perhaps she may not be at first so much mired." The duke she thought "great-souled," and it must ve been an occasion of great distress to her that her friend vift should not always share her views:

Madam [*he writes to her after failing to obtain some favour m Dorset*], I owe your Ladyship the acknowledgment of a ter I have long received, relating to a request I made to y Lord Duke. I now dismiss you, Madam, from your office being a go-between upon any affair I might have with his race. I will never more trouble him, either with my visits or plication. His business in this kingdom is to make himself sy; his lessons are all prescribed for him from Court; and is sure, at a very cheap rate, to have a majority of most rrupt slaves and idiots at his devotion. The happiness of is Kingdom is of no more consequence to him than it would to the Great Mogul ...

One wonders whether such suggestions troubled Lady tty. Was it possible that her great-souled friend would not Lord Steward and Lord Lieutenant of Ireland and Lord arden and Lord Lieutenant of Kent, did he not also happen be Duke of Dorset? Was it possible that people such as the ckvilles occasionally occupied positions due to their birth ther than to their intellect? Was it true that he, and parti-larly Lord George, cared for their own advancement rather an for the credit of England?—they who *were* England, who ared the blood of the Tudors and the Howards and the encers and the Cliffords? whose house was quarried from entish rock? whose oaks and beeches were rooted so deep to the soil of England? Lady Betty herself, who as Lady tty Berkeley had come from that most ancient castle—that se-and-grey castle, the colour of her own dried rose-leaves, e castle that, squat, romantic, and uncouth, brooded over e Severn across the meadows of Gloucestershire—Lady

Betty herself was of all people least qualified or likely
criticize. The household at Knole was ordered on a mag
ficent scale, with the duke and duchess and their guests at
apex of the pyramid which reposed on the base of five serva
at £20 each, two at £15, two at £10 10s., seven at £10, two
£8, thirteen at £6, eight at £5, two at £5, one at £2, besi
the chaplain who was unsalaried, the senior officers,
Steward, the Comptroller, and the Master of the Horse
£60, £30, and £25 respectively, Tom Durfey living over
dairy, and the rabble of labourers, gardeners, and what-not,
whom nobody took any notice. This was life as Lady Be
was accustomed to find it ordered. If ever she paused
question its system, no trace of her wondering appears in
letters.

She had a house of her own, Drayton, in Northamptonshi
considered by Horace Walpole, a "venerable heap of uglin
with many curious bits," which she had inherited from I
late husband, who in his turn had inherited it from a first wi
This husband of Lady Betty's is a peculiar figure; so peculi
indeed, so ambiguous, and so equivocal, that one wonders
his alliance with the orderly Lady Betty Berkeley, unless tl
may be explained by the fact that he "possessed a very han
some person, and was always a distinguished favourite of t
other Sex." He was, I gather, a soldier of fortune, of u
certain parentage, or, as Lord George Sackville delicately pt
it, "believed to stand in a very close degree of consanguin
to King William the Third." William, at any rate, broug
him over to England from Holland in 1688, knighted hi
saw to it that he became a member of the House of Commoi
and assisted him with grants of money; and Germain, w.
inherited from his father no armorial bearings, was accu
tomed to use a red cross, which might be taken to mean tl
his actual was higher than his ostensible birth. This gentl
man combined with the instincts of a collector a profou
ignorance of artistic matters. His principal pride was his co
lection of "Rarities," in which he would exhibit the dagg
of Henry VIII; he believed a certain Sir Matthew Germa
to be the author of St. Matthew's Gospel; and at Drayto

ere he was building a colonnade, he caused the columns to placed upside down, as he had mistaken the capitals for pedestals.

This was the man who married Lady Betty Berkeley when was thirty years younger than himself. He had previously n married to the Duchess of Norfolk, whose husband orced her on Sir John Germain's account. After her death, which he inherited Drayton, he attached himself to the ke and Duchess of Dorset, who received him with their ated hospitality; but this was not enough: he wanted a lliant alliance, he wanted an heir to Drayton. While at stol he "cast his eyes upon Lady Betty, whose birth, char-er, and accomplishments rendered her every way worthy his choice." They married; and the friendship with the rsets, to whom Lady Betty was already devoted, was engthened by the new bond. Although the difference in age s so considerable, Lady Betty, through her "superior under-nding, added to the most correct deportment, acquired at influence over him," and when after twelve years of rriage Sir John died, "a martyr to the gout as well as to er diseases," he called his wife to his bedside and spoke her in these terms:

Lady Betty [*said he*], I have made you a very indifferent sband, and particularly of late years, when infirmities have dered me a burden to myself, but I shall not be much ger troublesome to you. I advise you never again to marry old man, but I strenuously exhort you to marry when I am ne, and I will endeavour to put it in your power. You have filled every obligation towards me in an exemplary man-r, and I wish to demonstrate my sense of your merits. I ve, therefore, by my will, bequeathed you this estate, which received from my first wife; and which, as she gave to me, I leave to you. I hope you will marry and have children to herit it. But, if events should determine otherwise, it would ve me pleasure to think that Drayton descended after your cease to a younger son of my friend the Duchess of Dorset.

He then passed away, but in one particular Lady Betty did t take his advice: she never married again, although she

survived him by fifty years, and thus it is perhaps that I reg
her, with her crewel work, her china closet, and her p
pourri, rather as a spinster than as a widow. There is no tr
at all at Knole of Sir John Germain, that royal bastard, t
handsome and enterprising child of fortune, thanks to wh
Drayton came into the possession of Lord George and c
tinues to this day in the hands of his descendants. Of La
Betty, on the other hand, there are copious traces. There
her rooms, which I have already described in the first chap
her small square four-poster, her ring-box, and the pain
wooden figure of a lady with the *fontange* of Queen Ann
day on her head. There is Lady Betty's own portrait
miniature full-length, in blue brocade. There is yard up
yard of her industrious embroidery. There is the pot-pot
which is made every summer from her receipt (1750):

Gather dry, Double Violets, Rose Leaves, Lavend
Myrtle flowers, Verbena, Bay leaves, Rosemary, Balm, Mu
Geranium. Pick these from the stalks and dry on paper in t
sun for a day or two before putting them in a jar. This sho
be a large white one, well glazed, with a close fitting cover, a
a piece of card the exact size of the jar, which you must ke
pressed down on the flowers. Keep a new wooden spoon
stir the salt and flowers from the bottom, before you put i
fresh layer of bay salt above and below every layer of flowe
Have ready of spices, plenty of Cinnamon, Mace, Nutm
and Pepper and Lemon-peel pounded. For a large jar $\frac{1}{2}$
Orris root, 1 oz. Storax, 1 oz. Gum Benjamin, 2 ozs. Calami
Aromatico,[1] 2 grs. Musk, and a small quantity of oil
Rhodium. The spice and gums to be added when you ha
collected all the flowers you intend to put in. Mix all w
together, press it down well, and spread bay salt on the t
to exclude the air until the January or February followi
Keep the jar in a cool, dry place.

In the second respect Lady Betty carried out her husban
wishes, for when she died herself at the age of nearly nine
she bequeathed the "venerable heap of ugliness" to Lo
George, with £20,000 and half the residue of her estate.

[1] The powdered dried root of Sweet Sedge (*Acorus Calamus*).

§ iv

CHARLES SACKVILLE, 2nd Duke *of* Dorset

Since I have avoided all political details, which would have
[ ]d anyone more conversant than myself with the background
[ ] the facts into pages of dissertation, there remains very little
[ ] say of the first Duke of Dorset. He died a few years before
[ ]s dear, dear Colly, and was succeeded by his son, that Lord
[ ]iddlesex to whom I have alluded as being so unsatisfactory.
[ ]here is not much record of this good-for-nothing duke, who
[ ]joyed his dukedom only four years, and who was married
[ ] a "very short, very plain, very yellow, and vain girl, full of
[ ]reek and Latin." Apparently he married her no earlier than
[ ] need, for Horace Walpole writes of "Lord Middlesex's
[ ]edding, which was over a week before it was known. I
[ ]lieve the bride told it then, for he and all his family are so
[ ]ent that they would never have mentioned it; she might
[ ]ve popped out a child, before a single Sackville would have
[ ]en at the expense of a syllable to justify her." I have already
[ ]uoted the few epithets I have found relating to this duke, the
[ ]proud, disgusted, melancholy, solitary man . . ." who pro-
[ ]uced operas and spent enormous sums on defending singers
[ ] legal actions. He was reputed mad, "a disorder which there
[ ]as too much reason to suppose, ran in the blood"; he was
[ ]rtainly eccentric and there is a large picture of him in the
[ ]all-room at Knole dressed as a Roman emperor, with bare
[ ]ees, a plumed helmet on his head, and various pieces of
[ ]rmour. Besides these scanty documents, there are some
[ ]rses which scarcely entitle him to be called a poet: *Arno's*
[ ]*ale*, which I have never read, and which is addressed to a
[ ]rtain Madame Muscovita, whose portrait is at Knole; and
[ ]thers which are at Knole, for instance:

DUCK HUNTING

Hard by where Knole's exalted towers rise
Upon a green smooth plain a pond there lies,

With verdant grass encircled round, a place
Seated commodiously the duck to chase.
Here in the heat of day the youths for sport
With well-taught spaniels to the pond resort.
The youths on ev'ry side the pond surround,
With fav'ring cries the hollow woods resound.
The eager dogs with barking rend the skies
Until encouraged by their masters' cries
They plunge into the stream: the stream before 'em flies.
Rover, the first that plung'd, the first in fame
And one from Charles's noble breed that came.
The next came Trip, tho' of a bastard race,
And smaller size, he swam the next in place.
The last came Ranger, with his spotted back,
That swam but slow: the gravest of the pack.
His deep rough voice was of a hoarser sound
With long red ears that swept along the ground. . . .
And thus the sport goes on, till weary grown,
And ev'ryone is willing to go home.
The weary duck at last swims close to land;
They take her up with a kind, pitying hand.
Of every spannel they extoll the praise
And all their virtues to the skies they raise.
And then they, weary, homewards take their way,
And drown in sprightly bowls the labours of the day.

The duke's poems are worthless, of course, but among t
Knole papers of this date is one which I cannot forbear fro
reproducing:

AN EPISTLE *from* DAME I . . . L . . . *to the*

REVD. MR. B . . .

Sweet youth, 'tis hard thy innocence should be
A source of scandal and reproach to me.
Nay, blush not—with reluctance I pervail
O'er innate modesty to own the tale.

That fatal day when first I saw thy face
And marked each angel-look and smiling grace,
Thy fair idea struck my tender heart,

And, oh! remained, though thou didst soon depart;
Maternal love, methought, thou didst inspire,
Around my heart still played the lambent fire.
Thoughtless of harm, why should I aught conceal?
A friend I meet, and thus the truth reveal:

"Say, didst thou mark that dove-like form to-day,
Those eyes that languished with so mild a ray?
Can fleecy lambs such innocence disclose,
E'er glowed such blushes on the opening rose?
Safe could I take the youngster to my bed
And on my bosom fondly rest his head,
Harmless the tedious night were so beguiled;
So watch fond mothers o'er the sucking child."

That seeming friend betrayed me, and began
To whisper through the house, "I loved the man."
Then memory spread and worse suspicions rose,
And searching spies broke in on my repose;
Nor chamber, closet, bed, were sacred then:
They sought to find thee, ah! they sought in vain!
Thou wrapped in innocence might sleeping be,
Unconscious of the woes I bore for thee.

The uproar now withdrawn, I strive to rest,
And throw my arms across my pensive breast.
Soon as my eyelids close I see thy form,
Pure as the snow-drop, yet in blushes warm.
But oh! what followed?—strange effect of fright,
I dreamed that in my bed thou pass't the night . . .

Come, with thy innocence, thy smiles impart
Fresh joy to me, and mend each wicked heart,
Talk much of charity, and Love, *too, teach:*
'Tis mine to suffer, but 'tis thine to preach.

CHAPTER VIII

KNOLE AT THE END OF THE EIGHTEENTH CENTURY

JOHN FREDERICK SACKVILLE, 3rd Duke *of* Dorset

§ i

THE PORTRAIT by Gainsborough in the ball-room is of a m
with a curved mouth, deep grey eyes, and powdered h
brushed back off his forehead. He looks out from the oval
his framing, beautiful and melancholy. "I have always look
on him as the most dangerous of men," said the Duchess
Devonshire, "for with that beauty of his he is so unaffect
and has a simplicity and a persuasion in his manner that mak
one account very easily for the number of women he has h
in love with him." There is much in him which recalls h
forefather, Charles, the Dorset of the Restoration, but this i
personality less opulent, less voluminous, more wistful a
more romantic; all his accessories are essentially of t
eighteenth century—his Chinese page, his diamonds, h
scarf-pin, his Italian mistress who caused so much scandal
dancing at the Opera in Paris with his Garter bound about h
forehead. He is the immediate precursor of the generati
which replaced by Gothic the Tudor windows in the Orange
made serpentine some of the straight paths in the garden, a
decorated the windows in the Colonnade with representatio
of knights in full armour. He himself escaped the baron
tendencies. He belonged to an age more delicate, more e
quisite; an age of quizzing glasses, of flowered waistcoats,
buckled shoes, and of slim bejewelled swords. When he ha
his mistress sculpted, it was lying full length on a couch, nak
save for a single rose looping up her hair. When he had h
drawn, it was pointing her little foot in the first step of a danc
a tambourine in her hand, and the Chinese boy in the back
ground. When he wrote to his friends, it was in a bored, no

alant style, half in English and half in French. His manner
s "soft, quiet, and ingratiating." He treated the women
o loved him with an easy heartlessness which failed to
ninish their affection. He was possessed of no very great
ents other than those calculated to render life agreeable to him
the circles into which he was born, for it was his good fortune
be born handsome, rich, charming, and a duke, in a century
en those qualifications were a certain passport to success.

ohn Frederick Sackville became Duke of Dorset at the age
twenty-four. He was the son of that Lord John Sackville
o passes across the annals of the family early in life as a
et and cricketer, and later as a sad and shabby figure,
ways dirtily clad," living under mild restraint at Vevey, a
tim to melancholia. There was, however, no hint as yet of
s hereditary strangeness of temper in his son, the new Duke
Dorset. The young man came brilliantly into his new pos-
sions, paid the undertaker £66 6s. for the late duke's
eral, paid the Sheriff £418 2s. for "things taken at Knole"—
m which it would seem that the late duke had died in debt—
ught four thousand ounces of silver, and entertained his
ghbours and tenantry to a feast in celebration of his suc-
sion, at which sixty stone of beef, mutton, and veal were
nsumed, thirty-four pounds of wax-lights used, and
sicians provided. It is interesting to see how the price of
ne had altered between the days of Charles II and this time;
nely, 1769. Claret now cost 54s. a dozen, Burgundy 60s. a
zen, Champagne 97s. a dozen, and port for the servants'
le cost 20s. a dozen, in comparison with the few shillings
d per gallon a century earlier. The only thing which did not
e p. 134] alter in proportion is beer, for which 35s. a hogs-
d was paid in the seventeenth century and £2 10s. a hogs-
d in the eighteenth. The young duke's time, we are told,
s "devoted to gallantry and pleasure among the fashionable
cles as well in France and Italy as in England," a phrase
ich begins to acquire a fatally familiar ring through the
erations of the family. Perhaps nothing else could reason-
y be expected of him. Life offered him too great an ease
l too many advantages; why should he have rejected them?

Before he had been for a year in the enjoyment of his honou
and estates he had set out on the Grand Tour accompani
by the celebrated Nancy Parsons and a train of singers, acto
and Bohemians, who clustered round him in every Europe
capital which he visited. Echoes of his extravagance and
escapades come down to us from Paris and from Rome.
entertained lavishly every evening, inviting only those w
could amuse his already blasé appetite; he rescued his Nan
Parsons in the nick of time as she was about to be abduct
from a masked ball by a noble Venetian; he indulged his ta
for the fine arts "even beyond the limits of his fortune";
bought a Perugino, he bought a doubtful Titian, and a numb
of Italian primitives; he bought from a Mr. Jenkins in Ro
"the figure of Demosthenes in the act of delivering an oration
fine Grecian relick in marble," and a bronze cast of t
Gladiator Repellens, on whose shield he caused his own co
of-arms to be embossed. This kind of existence he continu
to lead for two or three years, when he threw over Nan
Parsons, returned to England, and became the lover of a M
Elizabeth Armistead. Meanwhile, it appears from his accou
books that large sums were being spent by his orders on bo
outdoor and indoor repairs at Knole. He put down new floo
altered some of the windows, and bought further enormo
quantities of silver, 5920 ounces in one year alone, costi
£2463 17s. 7d., and including a hundred and forty-four silv
plates, eight dozen each of forks, and spoons, dishes of
kinds, covers, and tureens. Occupied with Knole, love affai
and cricket, he dawdled away a particularly gilded yout
Details from his account-books give a good idea of his expens
and occupations:

	£	s.
Mrs. Gardiner, lace ruffles	41	0
Butler, new chain	80	0
Opera, expenses last winter	17	19
Opera, subscription	21	0
Paid Sir Joshua Reynolds	78	15

Mrs. Elizabeth Armistead reigned for three years, but th
duke had other diversions in other circles: the gay, frivolou

d wanton Lady Betty Hamilton, trailing from ball to ball
th her suitors in her wake, set her heart upon him, and he,
t unresponsive, was ready to trifle so long as he was not
pected to marry. Lady Betty was finally married off to Lord
erby, reputed the ugliest and the richest peer in England.

Many were the means employed till Lord Derby's constant
d assiduous care veiled the ugliness of his person before the
ol he worshipped. Time and despair made Lady Betty give
hasty and undigested consent. After a day of persecutions
om every quarter, while a hair-dresser was adorning her
happy head, she traced the consent with a pencil on a scrap
paper, and sent it wet with her tears to her mother.

re-shuffle now took place: the duke became the new Lady
erby's lover, and Lord Derby became the lover of Mrs.
rmistead. This arrangement, however, was not of long dura-
n. Lord Derby fell in love with Elizabeth Farren; Lady
erby, it was rumoured, ran away and had to be brought
ck by her brother, the Duke of Hamilton: still bent upon
arrying the Duke of Dorset, she wished to divorce Lord
erby, but was foiled by the prudence of Miss Farren. The
ssips of London were much excited by all these occurrences.
ady Sarah Lennox wrote: "It is no scandal to tell you it is
agined that the Duke of Dorset will marry Lady Derby.
am told she has been and still is most thoroughly attached
him." It would be satisfactory to know exactly what part
orset played; I fear not a very creditable one. Lady Derby
as an impulsive, headstrong, attractive creature, capable of
al passion under all her lightheartedness and easy virtue;
r husband was unfaithful to her; her rival more sage and
xperienced than she herself; her lover ready to take what he
uld without incurring an irksome responsibility. My grand-
ther's sister, Lady Derby, used to show at Knowsley the
indow through which the Duke of Dorset was reported to
ave been admitted to the house, disguised as a gardener, and
was commonly supposed that the infant Lady Elizabeth
tanley was in reality the duke's daughter. But when the
fair threatened to become too serious he was only too ready
 resume his travels abroad.

I can only suppose that it was during one of his absenc
that Horace Walpole went to Knole and found it not at all
his liking, for he draws a picture of the place in a state
desertion which would surely not have been warranted h
the duke and his household been in occupation:

I came to Knole [*he writes to Lady Ossory*], and that was
medley of various feelings! Elizabeth and Burleigh and Buc
hurst; and then Charles [*he means Richard*] and Anne, Dors
and Pembroke, and Sir Edward Sackville, and then a mc
engaging Dorset, and Villiers and Prior, and then the old du
and duchess, and Lady Betty Germaine, and the court
George II.

The place is stripped of its beeches and honours, and h
neither beauty nor prospects. The house, extensive as it
seemed dwindled to the front of a college, and has the silen
and solitude of one. It wants the cohorts of retainers, and t
bustling jollity of the old nobility, to disperse the gloom.
worship all its faded splendour, and enjoy its preservatio
and could have wandered over it for hours with satisfactio
but there was such a heterogenous housekeeper as poisoned
my enthusiasm. She was more like one of Mrs. St. John
Abigails than an inhabitant of a venerable mansion, an
shuffled about in slippers, and seemed to *admire* how I cou
care about the pictures of such old *frights* as covered the wal

§ ii

I have said that cricket as well as love affairs occupied tl
duke's time, and in this he was only carrying on the traditic
begun by his father and his uncle, who were both enthusiast
cricketers and took part in the first match recorded as havir
been played at Sevenoaks, in 1734, between Kent and Susse
Lord John Sackville and Lord Middlesex playing, of cours
for Kent. Six years later Sevenoaks played London on tl
famous Vine cricket ground at Sevenoaks—the first matc
recorded on the Vine. The young Duke of Dorset inherite
his father's taste, keeping in his employ professional crickete
such as Bowra, Miller, and Minskull, and we have endle
details of the matches played, an old print of one match takir

ce on the Vine between the duke's men and Sir Horace
ann's men, which shows the players all wearing jockey-caps
d finally a number of cricketing ballads, more noticeable
their enthusiasm than for their excellence:

> His Grace the Duke of Dorset came [we read],
> The next enrolled in skilful fame.
> Equalled by few, he plays with glee,
> Nor peevish seeks for victory,
> And far unlike the modern way
> Of blocking every ball at play,
> He firmly stands with bat upright
> And strikes with his athletic might,
> Sends forth the ball across the mead
> And scores six notches for the deed.

There is in particular a great contest between Kent and
rrey, celebrated in a ballad of sixty-five verses, in which

> The fieldsmen, stationed on the lawn,
>   Well able to endure,
> Their loins with snow-white satin vests
>   That day had guarded sure,

d it is related that in this match also the Duke of Dorset
s playing for the honour of his county, for we are told that

> Young Dorset, like a baron bold,
>   His jetty hair undrest,
> Ran foremost of the company,
>   Clad in a milk-white vest.

spite the efforts of the duke and the men of Kent, they
re defeated by Surrey, and the duke met with disaster:

> "O heavy news!" the Rector cried,
>   "The Vine can witness be,
> We have not any cricketer
>   Of such account as he."[1]

[1] This ballad is by John Duncombe, and is given in full in *Kentish
ets*, vol. II, p. 364 (1821).

It is satisfactory to learn that in the return match Surr was beaten.

§ iii

We come now to the period when "the gay Duke of Dors became ambassador in Paris," and "his encouragement of t Parisian ballet was the amazement and envy of his age." It entertaining, and rather sad, to read both his official despatch from Paris and his private letters to his friends, and to refle that while he was writing to the Duchess of Devonshire, suppose you will hear talk of my ball, it has made a great no at Paris"; or to the Foreign Office, "It is hardly possible conceive a moment of more perfect tranquility than t present, the French government, free from the late causes its anxiety, appears entirely bent upon improving the advan tages of peace,"—it is sad, and certainly ironical, to reflect th the taking of the Bastille was distant by a paltry three yea With no foreboding of those tremendous events, which mo than any war, more even than the career of Napoleon, were change the fortunes of humanity, the Court of France and t English envoy continued on their course of enjoyment. T Duke of Dorset became, naturally, extremely popular in Par He was himself not sure that he wholly liked the French:

All the French are *aimable, si vous voulez*, but they a capricious and inconstant, especially the women [*he wro home to the Duchess of Devonshire*]; in short, I have really friend here but Mrs. B. [Marie Antoinette], and then I s her so seldom that I forget half what I want to say to her. T Frenchmen are all jealous and treacherous, so that betwee the capriciousness of the fair sex and the want of confiden I have in the other *je me sens vraiment malheureux*, I assu you, my dearest duchess.

But the French had no corresponding fault to find. The En lish ambassador was princely and lavish; he was spendin money, as he himself admitted, at the rate of £11,000 a yea he was greatly in the Queen's favour, so greatly that he h been included by certain authorities (notably Tilly) in the

s of her lovers. Sir Nathaniel Wraxall, who, although an
accurate was yet a contemporary writer, says that this was
so, and that he has seen a letter-case, preserved by the
e, full of Marie Antoinette's notes addressed to him.
axall says that they were written on private concerns, com-
ssions that she requested him to execute for her, prin-
ally regarding English articles of dress or ornament, and
er innocent and unimportant matters. Whether Dorset
s or was not her lover is not of the smallest importance; and
ely no one would grudge, at this distance of time, any
asure that a princess so young and so unfortunate might
e enjoyed in life.

A question in which the Duke was naturally much inter-
ed was the affair of the diamond necklace. His despatches
the Foreign Office are full of references to the story, from
gust, 1785 onwards:

The usually credited account is, that the Cardinal [de
han] has forged an order from the Queen to the Jeweller
the Crown to deliver to him diamonds to the amount of
00,000 livres, and which diamonds he actually received.
hat makes this event the more extraordinary is that the
rdinal is known to be a man of extremely good parts, and
in the enjoyment of the greatest honour and revenues to
ich any subject in the Church can aspire.

d again:

Mme. de la Motte, from an apprehension that her life is in
nger, affects to have lost her senses. The jailer, upon enter-
g her room the day before yesterday, was some time before
discovered her, and at length found her under her bed,
ite naked.

It would take up too much space to give all Dorset's des-
tches on this subject. I mention them chiefly because a
ge proportion of the diamonds composing the original neck-
e is at Knole, one half having been purchased by the Duke
Dorset after the necklace had been split up and brought to
gland, and the other half by the Duke of Sutherland. This,

at least, is the tradition; and there is some evidence to sup
it, in a receipt among the Knole papers:

Received of his Grace the DUKE of DORSET nine hund
and seventy-five pounds for a brilliant necklace.
£975   For MR. JEFFERYS and self, WM JO

and this receipt is endorsed "Paid 1790," which tallies with
date when the necklace was sold by M. de la Motte to Jeffe
a jeweller in Piccadilly. They are beautiful diamonds, sm
but very blue, and are set at present in the shape of a tasseel
diadem.

Another topic which temporarily exercised the duke wl
in Paris was the "very extraordinary proposal" made to
French Government by a M. Montgolfier to

construct a balloon of a certain diameter to carry sixteen p
sons. The project [*the despatch continues*] is to carry on a tr
between this part and the South of France; Paris and M
seilles are the two places named. The balloon is to be freigh
with plate glass, and the return to be made in reams of pap
M. de Calonne has hitherto received the proposal with gr
coolness, as M. Montgolfier requires an advance of 60,c
livres Tournais. It is, however, under contemplation, as
Montgolfier has declared his intention of making the offer
our government in case he does not meet with encouragemo
here. It is said that the Comptroller General rather d
courages enterprises of this sort, as any further progress
the art of conducting balloons might tend to prejudice t
revenues of the City of Paris, which will shortly be su
rounded by a wall, the cost of which is estimated at four
five millions.

The duke naturally thought M. Montgolfier's pla
nonsensical:

I should almost scruple to mention to your Lordship
undertaking so extraordinary [*he says*] had I not heard fro
exceedingly good authority that such a plan is seriously
agitation. Great credit is given to M. Montgolfier's superi

ll in these matters, and that gentleman's friends are san-
ine in their expectations of his success. The weight he
poses to carry *exceeds that of a waggon-load!*

He gives some further details of what M. Montgolfier, who
retends to have at last discovered means of directing the
urse of Balloons," proposes to do:

He has obtained the sanction of M. de Calonne for his first
periment, which is to be made the first day of next May,
en he engages to depart from a town in Auvergne, distant
m Paris 150 miles, and to descend at or near this City in
e space of seven hours.

month later he writes:

The government has at last accepted M. Montgolfier's
oposal. 30,000 livres are to be granted to him in advance
the experiment, and if it succeeds the whole of his ex-
nses will be paid without any examination of his accounts,
pension granted to him, and every honorary recompense
stowed on him to which he can aspire. He pretends to have
scovered the means of guiding his machine, but it was not
l after his project to England, in case of refusal here, that it
as accepted.

On such topics as the diamond necklace and M. Montgolfier
d current affairs Dorset beguiled his leisure and that of the
oreign Office. There is no indication that he detected any
gns of the trouble in store. It is true that occasionally he
ites in this strain:

Their Majesties, the Dauphin, and the rest of the Royal
mily, are removed from Fontainebleau to Versailles. The
xpenses attending these journeys of the Court is incredible.
he duc de Polignac told me that he had given orders for
115 horses for this service. . . . Besides this, an adequate
roportion of horses are ordered for the removal of the heavy
aggage. . . . It is asserted that M de. Calonne will be under
e necessity of borrowing at least eight millions of livres next
ear,

and that after the fall of the Bastille he was moved to write:
really think it necessary that some public caution be gi
to put those upon their guard who may propose to visit t
part of the continent." But beyond these occasional comme
he does not seem to have been troubled by any thoughts of
future. He did not foresee that his friend "Mrs. B.," to wh
after his return to England he continued to supply Engl
gloves, would lose upon the scaffold that little head which h
carried so gaily the butterfly or the frigate, or that within t
or three years' time the English newspapers would be writi
"The Duke of Dorset's seat at Knole is a place of rendezvo
for the banished French *noblesse* at this time resident
England," or that he would be entertaining there as a fugit
his friend Champcenetz, a young officer in the Swiss Guar
and author of a "*Petit traité de l'amour des femmes pour
sots.*" Dorset would no doubt have proved a perfectly adequ
ambassador in normal times, but that vast situation with
infinite ramifications was beyond an intellect that accepted
granted the existing régime under which dukes were born
pleasure and labourers were not. But with all the foresight
the world it is difficult to see what he could have done, or h
the course of history could have been affected, had he se
home grave warnings instead of babbling of the diamo
necklace and M. Montgolfier.

There was another distraction for him in Paris: Gianne
Baccelli, an Italian dancer. The duke seems to have lost
head completely over her for the time being, for he gave h
his Garter to wear as a hair-ribbon, with "HONI SOIT Q
MAL Y PENSE" in diamonds, brought her home to England wi
him, sent her to a ball in Sevenoaks wearing the family jew
—which provoked a great scandal in the county—and gave h
one of the towers at Knole, which to this day remains, throu
the mispronunciation of the English servants, "Shelle
Tower". It was for this lady, or so the rumour ran, that
finally rejected the faithful and unfortunate Lady Derb
There was nothing that Dorset would not do for Bacce
Fanny Burney, visiting Knole with Mr., Mrs., and M
Thrale, writes that they were prevented from seeing t

ary and two or three other modernised rooms because
d^me Baccelli was not to be disturbed. The duke had her
ted by Reynolds, and painted and drawn by Gainsborough,
. sculpted from the nude. He even wrote to his friend the
chess of Devonshire asking her to do what she could for
protégée, "I don't ask you to do anything for her openly,"
wrote, "but I hope *que quand il s'agit de ses talents* you will
amend her. I assure you," he adds rather pathetically, "she
ne *bonne fille*, very clever, and *un excellent cœur*, and her
cing is really wonderful."

Gainsborough's large full-length portrait of Baccelli, origi-
y at Knole, has been sold; but his pencil sketch for it
ains, rather faded and very delicate of line. It is drawn in
ball-room: Baccelli stands on a model's throne, pointing
toe and lifting up her skirt; Gainsborough himself stands
ront of her, a palette in his hand, so that he turns his back
ards the person looking at the drawing; the Chinese page,
round hat, stands by. It reconstructs with great vividness
scene of her posing in the ball-room. The only pity is that
artist should not have drawn in the duke, who was surely
re, looking on, and criticising and making suggestions. The
eipt for the big picture is at Knole, though no mention is
de of the drawing.

Received of his Grace the DUKE of DORSET one hundred
neas in full for two ¾ portraits of his Grace, one full-length
Mad^sle Baccelli, two Landskips, and one sketch of a beggar
· and girl.
5   THOMAS GAINSBOROUGH, *June* 15, 1784.

One of the "two ¾ portraits of his Grace" mentioned in this
eipt is the one now in the ball-room, one of the most
utiful Gainsboroughs I know—included with five other
tures for the ludicrous sum of £105.

Reynolds' portrait of the dancer shows a mischievous and
active face, with slightly slanting eyes, peeping out from
ind a mask which she holds up in her hand. The duke even
it to the length of ordering the portraits of the servants he
provided for her, and among the collection of servants'

portraits in Black Boy Passage are Daniel Taylor and Eli
Law, servants of Mad^me Baccelli; Mrs. Edwards, attend
on Mad^me Baccelli; and Philip Louvaux, servant to Ma
Baccelli. She evidently, with her servants and her tower,
a regular establishment at Knole, and many receipts bea
her signature witness the duke's generosity towards
"Received 7th April 1786 of Mr. Burlington [the agent]
sum of fifty pounds on account of his Grace the Duke
Dorset, Jannette Baccelli," and so on. They had sev
children, all of whom died in babyhood, except one, allu
to in the following letter: "The duke has a very fine boy
whom Baccelli is mother, now at school near Knole. T
we think, is the only surviving progeny of the alliance,"
much as I should like to know, I have no idea what becam
this romantically-begotten scion, or even of whether he li
to grow up.

Perhaps the "heterogenous housekeeper" of Horace W
pole's letter was Baccelli's importation, for in another pl
he writes disgustedly of "Knole, which disappointed me mu
But unless you know how vast and venerable I though
remembered it, I cannot give you the measure of my surpr
but then there was a trapes of a housekeeper, who, I suppo
was the Baccelli's dresser, and who put me out of humour .

The connection seems to have lasted for a long time, fo
is not until the end of 1789 that we come across an old ne
paper cutting announcing with curious candour that "
Duke of Dorset and the Baccelli have just separated, and
is said to have behaved very well," so that she eclipsed
records of Nancy Parsons, of Mrs. Elizabeth Armistead,
of poor Lady Derby. It is, I think, a not unpicturesque in
dent in the story of Knole—the dancer sitting in those stat
rooms to Reynolds and Gainsborough, or descending fr
her tower to walk in the garden with the duke, attended by
Chinese boy carrying her gloves, her fan, or her para
Those were the days when the Clock Tower, oddly recall
a pagoda, was but newly erected; when the great rose-and-g
Chinese screen in the Poets' Parlour was new and brillian
the sun; when the Coromandel chests were new toys; and

Italian pictures and the statuary brought back by the duke from Rome were still pointed out as the latest acquisitions. And no doubt then the statue of the Baccelli reposing in her lovely nudity on her couch was not relegated to the attic, where a subsequent and more prudish generation sent it, but stood somewhere in the living-rooms, where it might be seen and admired in the presence of the smiling model. Amusement was caused, too, no doubt, among the guests of the duke and the dancer by Sir Joshua's portrait of the Chinese boy squatting on his heels, a fan in his hand, and the square toes of his red shoes protruding from beneath his robes. It was more original to have a Chinese page than to have a black one; everybody had a black one: "Dear Mama," wrote the Duchess of Devonshire to her mother, "George Hanger has sent me a black boy, eleven years old and very honest, but the duke don't like me having a black, and yet I cannot bear the poor wretch being ill-used; if you liked him instead of Michel I will send him, he will be a cheap servant and you will make a christian of him and a good boy; if you don't like him they say Lady Rockingham wants one." But the black page at Knole, of which there had always been one since the days of Lady Anne Clifford, and who had always been called John Morocco regardless of what his true name might be, had been replaced by a Chinaman ever since the house steward had killed the John Morocco of the moment in a fight in Black Boy's Passage. This particular Chinese boy whom I have mentioned, whose real name was Hwang-a-Tung, but whom the English servants, much as they called Baccelli Madam Shelley, more conveniently renamed Warnoton—fell on fortunate days when he came to Knole, for not only was he painted by Sir Joshua, but he was educated at the duke's expense at the Grammar School in Sevenoaks.

§ iv

The year after the parting in which the Baccelli was reported to have behaved so well, the duke married. His bride was an heiress, Arabella Diana Cope, of Bramshill who brought the

duke, according to his own statement, a dowry of £140,0
She must have been an imposing figure, if one may tr
Hoppner's portrait, which shows her walking in a white mus
dress, a little dog frisking round her feet, and tall feathers
her head; and Wraxall, who certainly knew her, says, with t
touch of awe and even dislike perceptible between the lines
all his accounts of her, that "her person, though not feminir
might then be denominated handsome; and, if her mind w
not highly cultivated or refined, she could boast of intellect
endowments that fitted her for the active business of life
Wraxall writes, possibly, with a prejudiced pen, for at o
time he was employed in sorting and classifying the Kn
manuscripts, and in this matter his views clashed with th
of her Grace and her Grace's second husband; the busine
was abandoned half-way through, but Wraxall's trace remai
in the neat, ejaculatory notes which I find on the reverse si
of many of the papers—"curious!" or "not without merit
This may account for the subtle spitefulness of his remar
Nevertheless, I imagine that Knole perceived under t
duchess' régime a considerable contrast with the days of t
merry and pleasure-loving Baccelli. The new duchess was
severe and orderly lady, "under the dominion of no passi
except the love of money, her taste for power and pleasu
always subordinate to her economy," and the duke himse
perhaps under the influence of his wife, began to turn fro
his extravagant ways towards parsimony, curtailing h
expenses in spite of the enormous increase in his income, a
becoming, moreover, irascible, fretful, morbid, and quarre
some. The days of his patronage of opera and Parisian ball
were over, the days when he was confident that the talk of h
ball in Paris would reach the ears of the Duchess of Devo
shire in London. His expenses at Knole were reported to
reduced to four or five thousand a year, yet he could n
endure to hear the praise of other houses, for Knole
considered "as possessing everything." It is not an attracti
picture of the gay duke's declining years. Hoppner, who ha
been staying at Knole for nine or ten days painting the thr
children, described the duke as most unpleasant in his tempe

xious and saving, humoursome and uncomfortable, "not
fering the dinner to be all placed on the table," and when,
ying at Casino, he lost fifteen shillings to Hoppner he
etted when the cards he wished for were taken up." The
ee children were brought up with the utmost severity; they
re scarcely allowed to speak in the presence of their elders;
d little Lord Middlesex was sent out of the room in disgrace
luncheon for asking his sister for the salt. Yet I fancy that
real control, under a show of submission, was exercised
that commanding figure, the duchess. She never betrayed
y signs of exasperation, whether the duke sent away the
iner, or grumbled that Neckar was a man of no family, or
it Mr. Hailes, the secretary, was a man of no family either
much to Mr. Hailes' discomposure. This dwelling upon
nily was one of his many crotchets, and he was fond of
inting out that the Sackvilles had never branched, but
nained the only family of that name in the Kingdom, and
uld draw attention to the coincidence that Sackville Street
s the longest street in London without branch or turning.
udent and long-suffering, no doubt the duchess had in her
nd the advantages she intended to secure when she should
no longer a wife and sick-nurse, but a widow. Baccelli's
tue was in the attic, and Mr. Ozias Humphrey, of the Royal
ademy, was quite out of favour because he went to Knole
the duke's absence and took possession of a room without
eviously showing proper attention to the duchess. She
esided calmly, while the duke fretted and economized, and
arrelled with his friends, and deteriorated in intellect, and
came a prey to gloom, and grew old and sad before his time;
e presided unruffled, for all the while she rested satisfied in
r knowledge of his testamentary dispositions. He was, in fact,
hough only in the fifties, already a very ill man. He was
ling rapidly into a deeper and deeper melancholy, and there
a tradition that towards the end he could only be soothed by
e playing of two musicians in a neighbouring room—the
om now called the Music Room, in which hang, rather
nically, Reynolds' portrait of the Baccelli peeping out from
hind her mask, and Vigée Lebrun's portrait of the grave,

grey-haired lady, Arabella Diana, Duchess of Dorset. He
in the library, his hands fumbling at the breast-pin in
jabot, while the soothing strains reached him, veiled
distance. Veiled by distance, too, the memories of his p
floated to him on the music, and melted with the music i
the solace of a confused and wistful harmony. The past,
luminous, was not wholly lost, since in memory it was s
recoverable. There had been the fun of the masked ball
Rome; there had been the clandestine hours of tenderness w
Betty Hamilton; there had been Versailles; there had been t
days when he could glance down through the window a
see Baccelli flirting with Sir Joshua on the lawn. The musicia
in the neighbouring room played on. He had been twent
four when Knole had come to him; he had not had to wait
his good things until he was grown too sober to enjoy the
It had been so easy to accept the urbanity, the *empresseme*.
everyone was eager to lavish; so pleasant to move in a wor
so bland, so obliging, and so polite. No effort had be
necessary; the fat quails had dropped ready roasted into
mouth. No effort: a smile there; a gracious word here; toss
alike with a casual, if good-humoured, contempt. Surveyi
himself in his mirror while his valet knelt to buckle t
diamond Order round his knee, flicking with a lace pocke
handkerchief at a few grains of powder fallen upon his co
he had been secure in the safe conduct of his great name a
his personal charm. And if the faint ghosts whispered rou
him now in the quiet library at Knole—a fair head thrust
him upon a pike, the reproachful eyes of Lady Derby, t
stilled limbs of those half-Italian babies that the Baccelli ha
borne him—why, he could banish them: Lord Middles
slept in his nursery upstairs, and the tall duchess watche
effaced though vigilant, from a corner of the library. B
when she rose and came towards him, thinking that he ha
fallen asleep in his nodding over the fire, he repulsed her fre
fully, with the gesture of an old man, and wondered at hims
in his confused and unhappy mind for this anomalous di
courtesy towards a woman.

There is a sad little comment on the early deterioration

e gay duke. He was only 40 years old when Fanny Burney
ote:

"Well," she (the Queen) continued, "so there was standing
me a man that I could not see in the face, but I saw the
isting of his brow; and I said to Lady Harcourt, 'I am sure
at must be nobody but the Duke of Dorset.' 'Dear,' she says,
ow can you tell that?' 'Only ask,' said I, and so it proved he."
"Yes," cried the King, "he is pretty well again; he can smile
ain now!"

It seems his features had appeared to be fixed, or stiffened.
is said, that he has been obliged to hold his hand to his
outh, to hide it, ever since his stroke—which he refuses to
knowledge was paralytic.

The Queen looked as if some comic notion had struck her,
d, after smiling a little while to herself, said, with a sort of
nocent archness, very pleasing, "To be sure, it is very wrong
laugh at such things—I know that; but yet, I could not
lp thinking, when his mouth was in that way, that it was
ry lucky people's happiness did not depend upon his smiles."

It seems very odd indeed that he should have been retained
our Ambassador in Paris after this calamity had overtaken
m, but in those undemocratic days it was perhaps more
portant to be a duke than a competent representative of
e's country.

Next door to the Music Room hangs the lovely full-length
the three children, painted by Hoppner while on that
comfortable visit.[1] One is bound to admit that their appear-
ce bears no impress of the grand, solemn, and gloomy
usehold in which they were being brought up. The little
y, rosy, flaxen-curled, in high nankeen trousers and a soft
lly shirt, has his arms round his baby sister, who, with bare
es, is looking sulkily at her elder sister's shoes. They are out
the park; nothing could be more natural or unconstrained.
y grandfather used to show me the baby girl, his mother,
ling me that while Hoppner was seeking for a pose for his
cture a grievance arose between the two little girls because

[1] Alas, no longer now. It was bought by Mr. Thomas Lamont,
w York.

one had shoes and the other had not, and that their brot
took his sister into his arms for consolation, whereup
Hoppner rushed at them exclaiming that he could not impre
upon the charm of this accidental pose. I think this story '
a convincing ring about it. Certainly it was the only anecd
which my grandfather had to tell of any picture in the hou
usually he did not know a Hoppner from a Vandyck, a Knel
from a Gainsborough. He said that he had the story strai
from his mother, Lady Elizabeth, the sulky baby of Hoppne
picture, and the young woman in fancy dress of Beeche
portrait in the same room.

The only pleasant aspect of these later years of the gay duk
life is his friendship and constant employment of the artists
his day. Before he fell into what Wraxall calls his "men
alienation" he counted Reynolds among his intimates, wa
pall-bearer at his funeral in Westminster Abbey, and accun
lated so many works of that artist at Knole, including one
the back of which is written, "Sir Joshua Reynolds, pain
by himself and presented to his Grace the Duke of Dorset
1780," that what was once the Crimson Drawing-Roo
became known as the Reynolds Room; and the Reyno
Room it is to this day. Madame Vigée Lebrun stayed at Kno
which she found too gloomy for her taste, the duchess warni
her, the first time they sat down to dinner, "You will find
very dull, for we never speak at table." Ozias Humphr
before he was so unfortunate as to offend the duchess, co
tributed a number of canvases to the duke's collection:

Two pastels, 12 guineas each.

KNIGHTSBRIDGE, *June 25th,* 17

	£	s.
His Grace the Duke of Dorset to Ozias Humphrey, for a portrait in miniature	16	16
A small crayon picture of the crossing-sweeper at Hyde Park Corner with a rich gold frame and glass	21	0
A portrait of the Duchess of Dorset in crayons	12	12
	£50	8

Received of his Grace the Duke of DORSET the sum of
ty pounds in full for the amount of the annexed bill.

OZIAS HUMPHREY.

It is perhaps significant of his new economy that the duke
nored the eight shillings.

With Opie, too, he was on friendly terms, and amongst the
her receipts at Knole is one from Opie for the portrait of
lmund Burke for £24 3s. There is also a letter at Knole from
irke, who probably knew his Grace's weakness for his house:

y LORD,   DUKE ST., *Sept.* 14, 1791.
I am just now honoured with your Grace's letter, and am
tremely concerned that it is not in my power to accept your
race's most obliging invitation. I have great respect for its
esent possessor; and as for the place, I, who am something
a lover of all antiquities, must be a very great admirer of
nole. I think it the most interesting thing in England. It is
easant to have preserved in one place the succession of the
veral tastes of ages; a pleasant habitation for the time, a
and repository of whatever has been pleasant at all times.
his is not the sort of place which every banker, contractor,
Nabob can create at his pleasure. . . . I would not change
nole if I were the Duke of Dorset for all the foppish structures
this age.

Other receipts at Knole make it clear that the average price
r a half-length was £37, while for a full-length by Reynolds
e duke paid £300.

There is also a mention in a contemporary diary that the
ıke asked Hoppner for his portrait, which he promised
ould be hung next to Sir Joshua's portrait of himself. The
ary notes that Ozias Humphrey's *Selbstbildnis* is "still in the
om, but has been removed from its place next the Reynolds."
is "still in the room" now, a man with a delicate face and a
ıinted nose, on the wall with Gainsborough's *Lord George*
ıckville, Sir Joshua's *Samuel Foote*, his *Oliver Goldsmith*, his
g *Woffington*, and his own portrait; but the Hoppner for
hich the duke asked is not there, and never was; no doubt

Hoppner was not sufficiently encouraged by the uncomforta'
visit to send so valuable an acknowledgment.

At this period England lay under the fear of an invasion
the young victorious Bonaparte, and a scheme was set on fo
for raising a corps of infantry to be called the Knole volu
teers; I came across some of their accoutrements in an o
locker at Knole; they had an amateurish look. A docume
bearing many blots and the signatures of all the volunteers—
in some cases, their mark—is also at Knole:

HIS GRACE *the* DUKE *of* DORSET'S offer of raising a Corps
Infantry, to consist of Sixty Men, to be called the *Kn*
Volunteers, for the purpose of preserving Order and protecti
property in the Parish and Neighbourhood of Sevenoa
having been accepted, and George Stone, Stephen Woodga
and Thomas Mortimer Kelson being appointed officers I
his Majesty to command the same, they propose the followi
Rules and Regulations, which they hope will be cheerful
submitted to by all who have voluntarily come forward to off
their services in the said Corps at this important Crisis:

1st.   *That* each individual attend twice a week for the pu
         pose of exercising from half after Six o'clock to ha
         after Eight o'clock in the Evening.
2nd.   As a regular attendance is particularly essential, it
         proposed that the small Sum of Sixpence be paid b
         every person not present to answer to his Name whe
         called over at the time appointed, unless it appea
         he is prevented by Sickness, which forfeits, shou
         there be any, shall be spent by the Corps at the er
         of the year in any manner they shall think proper.
3rd.   That every Man appears clean and proper
         accoutered.
4thly.   That they do their utmost Endeavour to learn the
         Exercise, paying proper respect to their Officers.

Finally, they wish it to be clearly understood that the
Services shall not be required to extend further than the Paris
and Neighbourhood of Sevenoaks, unless it be for the purpos
of guarding Prisoners or Convoys as far as one Stage.

KNOLE, 22 *May*, 179

But it is improbable that the duke had much to do with the
[ri]sing or organization of this corps, for during the last
[tw]enty months of his life his irascibility turned to definite
[m]elancholia, and he remained at Knole more or less alone
[wi]th the duchess keeping a jealous guard over him. It is
[im]possible not to draw the parallel between his end and that of
[Ch]arles the Restoration earl, his great-grandfather, remember-
[in]g especially the wildness and extravagance in which both
[ha]d spent their youth; but whereas Charles was carried away
[to] Bath at the end by that sordid woman Ann Roche, the duke
[wa]s carefully tended in his own great house by the reserved
[an]d prudent woman he had married, too dignified to be accused
[sa]ve under the veil of polite phrases of intriguing to get the
[co]ntrol of his affairs into her own hands. So he sank gradually,
[an]d when in 1799, at the age of fifty-four, he died, it was
[fo]und that he had so disposed of his lands, his fortune, and his
[bo]roughs that Arabella Diana was left with so great an
[ac]cumulation of wealth and of parliamentary influence as had
[s]carcely ever vested, among us, in a female, and a widow."

FOOTNOTE: The Knole Volunteers inevitably suggest another
[vo]lunteer body, called into being nearly 150 years later, when another
[in]vasion threatened our island—the Home Guard. The old muskets
[an]d flint-locks were then lifted down from their racks at Knole, and
[ser]ved out to the empty-handed recruits, though it is hard to con-
[cei]ve what possible use they could have been against Hitler's advancing
[arm]y.
England is always very much the same.

CHAPTER IX

KNOLE IN THE NINETEENTH CENTURY

§ i

THE NEW Duke of Dorset was only five years old when his father's dignities descended so prematurely on to his sm... yellow head, but he had a capable mentor in the person of his mother, and before two years had elapsed her authority w... reinforced by that of a stepfather. This was Lord Whitwor... recently Ambassador to the Courts of Catherine II and Paul... The circumstances of Lord Whitworth's recall had been... the last degree mysterious. Various rumours were curre... amongst others, that he had offended the Czar in the followi... somewhat ludicrous manner: the Czar having forbidden th... any empty carriage should pass before a certain part of ... palace, Lord Whitworth, uninformed of the regulatio... ordered his coach to meet him at a point which would ent... passing over the forbidden area. The sentry held up the coac... the servants persisted in driving on; they came to blows; a... the Czar, when the affair came to his ears, ordered Lord Wh... worth's servants to be beaten, the horses to be beaten, and t... coach to be beaten too. Lord Whitworth, in a fit of rage a... petulance, dismissed his servants, ordered the horses to ... shot, and the coach to be broken into pieces and thrown in... the Neva.

He appears to have had at least one trait in common wi... the Sackvilles themselves, at any rate in early life, for it w... said of him that he was "more distinguished during this peri... of his career by success in gallantries than by any professio... merits or brilliant services." Even at the time of his marria... when, returning from Russia to England, he found availab... the wealthy and desirable relict of his friend the late Dors... he was heavily entangled with a lady named Countess Ge... betzow, whose partiality for the English Ambassador had be... such that she had placed her own fortune at his disposal ...

purpose of clothing himself and defraying the expenses of household. In return for this affection and assistance Lord itworth promised her marriage as soon as she could divorce husband; but during the course of the divorce proceedings Ambassador was recalled, and left for England on the lerstanding that Countess Gerbetzow would follow him re as soon as she conveniently could. Meanwhile he made acquaintance of the more eligible duchess, became en-ed to her, and lost no time in marrying her. Countess rbetzow had, however, by now obtained her divorce, and s travelling across Europe on her way to England: at Leip-she learnt from a newspaper that Lord Whitworth in ndon was engaged to the Duchess of Dorset. Indignant and raged, she flew post-haste to London. Too late: she arrived y to find that the marriage had already been celebrated. t she would not allow the matter to rest there, and "her lamations, which were of too delicate and serious a nature be despised, at length compelled the duchess, most reluct-ly, to pay her Muscovite rival no less a sum than ten usand pounds." Whether the duchess continued to think rd Whitworth worth the price is not recorded. If he was an ensive husband, he was certainly from the worldly stand-nt a very successful one, and that was a standpoint the chess was not likely to despise. He became successively bassador to the French Republic, Lord Lieutenant of land, and an earl, but "we may nevertheless be allowed doubt," observes Wraxall, who claims Lord Whitworth's sonal friendship,

ether a humbler matrimonial alliance might not have been ended with more felicity . . . united to a woman of inferior tune and condition . . . he would certainly have presented object of more rational envy and respect than as the second sband of a duchess, elevated by her connections to dig-ies and offices, subsisting on her possessions, and who will bably ere long inter him with an earl's coronet on his fin.—I return [*says Wraxall, having thus dismissed the pair*] Marie Antoinette.

I doubt whether the little duke was allowed a very exuberant

enjoyment of his boyhood with this couple in authority o
him. Children were strictly brought up in that generati
and it is clear that the duchess was by nature a severe and
very sympathetic woman. The little boy and his sisters m
have been docile and well behaved in the great house a
gardens which belonged to him in name only, but which
practice were entirely under his mother's control, for her
alter the windows as she pleased, and to put Lord Whitwort
cognizance in the stained glass beside the Sackville arms
visualize—I scarcely know why—the duchess and Lord Wh
worth almost as the jailers of the small inheritor. There
nothing to justify such a theory; and, indeed, very little rec
remains of that short life: there is his rocking-horse—
angular, long-necked, maneless animal, which in due cou
became my property, after passing through the two int
vening generations—his brief friendship with Byron a
schoolboy, and his portrait as a tall, fair young man in d
blue academical robes. There is very little else to mark
passage across the stage of Knole. He came, late in time,
a race never remarkable for strength of character, and
obituary notice which described him as having posses
gentle and engaging manners, tinctured by shyness, and
amiable temper, probably came nearer to the truth than
generality of such eulogies. Byron has told us nothing in
least illuminating of his friend. He has left a long address
verse, included in *Hours of Idleness*, in which he is careful
explain that the duke was his fag at Harrow,

> *Whom still affection taught me to defend,*
> *And made me less a tyrant than a friend,*
> *Though the harsh custom of our youthful band*
> *Bade* thee *obey, and gave* me *to command,*

and equally careful to remind him that they might in la
years meet in the House of Lords,

> *Since chance has thrown us in the self-same sphere,*
> *Since the same senate, nay, the same debate,*
> *May one day claim our suffrage for the state.*

he rest of the poem is an exhortation to the duke, whose
passive tutors, fearful to dispraise," may

> *View ducal errors with indulgent eyes,*
> *And wink at faults they tremble to chastise,*

be worthy of the record his ancestors have left him; of he
who "called, proud boast! the British drama forth," and of
that other one, Charles, "The pride of princes, and the boast
of song"—to become, in fine, "Not Fortune's minion, but her
blest son." One suspects, in fact, that Byron himself viewed
the errors of his ducal fag with an indulgent eye, and the depth
of the friendship, on Byron's part at least, is easily measured
by the letters he wrote on hearing of the duke's death—letters
whose cynicism is perhaps atoned for by their frankness:

I have just been—or, rather, ought to be—very much
shocked by the death of the Duke of Dorset [*he wrote to Tom
Moore*]. We were at school together, and then I was passion-
ately attached to him. Since, we have never met—but once, I
think, in 1805—and it would be a paltry affectation to pretend that I had any feeling for him worth the name. But there
was a time in my life when this event would have broken my
heart; and all I can say for it now is that—it is not worth
breaking.
Adieu—it is all a farce.

And he alludes to it once more, a fortnight later, again
writing to Moore, to say that "the death of poor Dorset—and
the recollection of what I once felt, and ought to have felt
now, but could not," has set him pondering.

That, then, is all which the boy could leave behind him—
that he should set Byron, for a moment, pondering. From such
slight traces—the English little boy of the Hoppner, the old-
fashioned rocking-horse, and the portrait of the fair young
man—we have to reconstruct as best we can an entire personality. We have to figure him running about the garden at
Knole; kissing his mother's hand—surely never throwing his
arms about her—his grave little bow to Lord Whitworth; the
"your Grace" of his nurse's behests; the brief contact with
the dazzling personality of Byron at Harrow; the stir with

which he cannot have failed to anticipate the advantages of
life and his emancipation. We have the account of him playi
tennis, when a ball hit him in the eye, and obliged him to
for ever after "continually applying leeches and blisters a
ointments and other disagreeable remedies," and to be "ve
moderate in all exercises that heat or agitate the frame."
have, finally, his tragic end at the age of twenty-one, to whi
additional poignancy is lent by the fact that he had recen
become engaged.

He had gone to Ireland, where his stepfather was th
Viceroy, to stay with his friend and quondam school-fell
Lord Powerscourt. On the day after his arrival the two you
men, with Lord Powerscourt's brother, Mr. Wingfield, we
out hunting, and after a fruitless morning they were about
return home when they put up a hare:

The hare made for the inclosures on Kilkenny Hill. Th
had gone but a short distance, when the Duke, who was
excellent forward horseman, rode at a wall, which was in fa
a more dangerous obstacle than it appeared to be. . . . T
Duke's mare attempted to cover all at one spring, and clear
the wall, but, alighting among the stones on the other sid
threw herself headlong, and, turning in the air, came wi
great violence upon her rider, who had not lost his seat;
undermost, with his back on one of the large stones, and s
crushing him with all her weight on his chest, and struggli
with all her might to recover her legs. The mare at length d
entangled herself and galloped away. The Duke sprang up
his feet, and attempted to follow her, but soon found hims
unable to stand, and fell into the arms of Mr. Farrel, who h
run to his succour, and to whose house he was conveye
Lord Powerscourt, in the utmost anxiety and alarm, rode f
speed for medical assistance, leaving his brother, Mr. Win
field, to pay every possible attention to the Duke. But, u
fortunately, the injury was too severe to be counteracted
human skill; life was extinct before any surgeon arrived. Su
was the melancholy catastrophe that caused the untimely dea
of this young nobleman. He had been of age only thr
months, and had not taken his seat in the House of Lor
[1815].

'he author of this obituary notice was at great pains to clear
young man of any charge of "unseasonable levity":

t has been said [*he observes*] that the Duke, in his dying
ments, made use of the expression "I am off." He did so;
 not, as has been very erroneously supposed, by way of
oic bravado, or in a temper of unseasonable levity; but
ply to signify to his attendants, who, in pulling off his
ts, had drawn him too forward on the mattress, and jogged
 of the chairs out of its place, that he was *slipping off*, and
ted their aid to help him up into his former position. He
 the last person in the world to be guilty of anything like
ty upon any solemn occasion, much less in his dying
ments. The fact was, when he used the expression "I am
' he had become very faint and weak, and was glad to save
self the trouble of further utterance. . . .

Now suppose a stranger to the real character of this ex-
ent youth to have heard no more of him than what he would
most likely to hear of one whose constitutional modesty
cealed his virtues, namely, that he was very fond of cricket,
t he hurt his eye with a tennis-ball, that he lost his life
ting, that his last words were "I am off"; would not a
son possessed of this information, and no more, naturally
clude that the Duke was a young man of trivial mind,
icted to idle games and field sports, and apt to make light
erious things? How false a notion would such a person form
he late Duke of Dorset! As to the four circumstances above
ded to, if he was fond of cricket, it was in the evening
erally that he played. When he hurt his eye [it was on the
 of December] he had been at his books all the morning,
 went between dinner and dusk to take one set at tennis.
en he lost his life hunting, he had not hunted ten times the
ole season. And what have been represented as his last
rds were not his last words; and, even if they were, they
 no other meaning than "Pray prevent a helpless man from
ping down out of his place." That he was not a mere
rtsman, a mere idler, or a mere trifler, witness the wet eyes
t streamed at every window in the streets of Dublin as his
rse was passing by; witness the train of carriages that com-
ed his funeral procession; witness the throng of Nobility
 Gentlemen that attended his remains to the sea-shore;
ness the families he had visited in Ireland; witness the

reception of his corpse in England; witness the amazing c
course of friends, tenantry, and neighbours, that came to l
the last rites performed, and to see him deposited in the to
witness the more endeared set of persons who still mea
hover round the vault where he is laid!

§ ii

It now became apparent how exceedingly wise had been
precautionary measures taken by the duchess in regard to
husband's will. A distant cousin, the son of Lord Geo.
succeeded to the title as fifth and last duke—this part of
succession was beyond the reach of her control—but un
the terms of the will Knole became her property for life,
she received in addition, on the death of her son, an incre
in her income of nine thousand a year. She must certa
have been one of the richest women in England. Lord W
worth, meanwhile (till 1817), continued as Lord Lieuten
of Ireland, and as the originals of the following letters writ
to him by Sir Robert Peel, with enclosures in Peel's ha
writing, are at Knole, I think it not wholly irrelevant to p
them here, with a few other notes, in view of their interes
being written immediately after the battle of Waterloo, a
having, so far as I know, never before been published.

Private   IRISH OFFICE.

DEAR LORD WHITWORTH,   *June 22nd, 18*

You will receive by this express the official accounts
the most desperate and most important action in which
British arms have ever been engaged. The Gazette details
the leading particulars—I have just been at the War a
Foreign Offices to collect any further information that n
be interesting to you. It is evident that the attack was i
great degree a surprise upon the Allies, Bonaparte collec
his troops and advanced with much greater rapidity t
could have been expected. It was supposed that it would ha
required three days to bring the British force into line fo
general engagement—but the suddenness of the attack g

em a much shorter time for preparation. It is said that on
e 16th the Prussians lost fourteen thousand men.

All the private accounts attribute the success of the day to
e Duke of Wellington's personal courage and extraordinary
ertions. Flint will send you some interesting particulars on
is point.

When the French Cavalry charged—the Duke placed him-
f in the centre of the square of infantry—a barrier that was
penetrable. Nothing could exceed the desperation with
iich the Cuirassiers fought. When they found they could
ake no impression on the solid mass of infantry—they
lted in front and deliberately charged their pistols and shot
individuals of course without a chance of surviving. Lord
thurst showed me a letter which he had received from
osley. He says that Bonaparte had a scaffolding erected out
cannon shot from the top of which he saw the field of battle
d the progress of the fight. When he found that success was
most hopeless he put himself at the head of the Imperial
uard—and charged in person. They were met by the first
ot guards who overthrew them completely. The conduct
all the British infantry was beyond praise—Lord Wellington
d about sixty-five thousand men in the field. Castlereagh
ld me that he thought Bonaparte must have lost the fourth
his army. This is of course mere conjecture.

Of the Regiments of Cavalry which distinguished them-
lves the Life Guards, the 10th, and the 18th are particularly
entioned. The field of battle after the action presented a
ost extraordinary sight. The panic of the French army after
eir failure—and the fruitlessness of the desperate courage
ey had shewn—was very great when the attack on our part
mmenced. They threw away their arms—knapsacks, etc.,
c., in the greatest confusion. The Prussians gave no quarter
the pursuit.

The Duke and Blucher met for a moment after the action—
the village of *La heureuse Alliance* [sic].

The Belgian Cavalry and some of the British did not much
istinguish themselves. I hear that the 7th, Lord Uxbridge's
wn regiment, have not added much to their reputation—but
o not quote me for this piece of intelligence. General Picton
as shot through the head. He behaved with the greatest
ossible gallantry.

Schartzenburg [sic] is supposed to have crossed the Rhine

with an immense force—perhaps 200,000 men on or abo
the 20th. I should rather say it was expected that he wou
cross about that time. There is no account from Paris—
from the French army.

I have sent you a strange mixture of detached and u
connected particulars. I heard them one by one—in such
hurry—and am now obliged to write to you in such a hur
that I may not detain the express that I cannot reduce the
into any shape.

The consequence of our success must infallibly lead to
reduction of our regular force in Ireland—forthwith I appr
hend. The Duke entreats in the strongest manner th
reinforcements of infantry may be sent to him.

Believe me ever

dear Lord Whitworth,

Yours most truly

The Lord Lieutenant.   ROBERT PEE

PARIS

Rue de la Paix—Hotel du Montblanc—

July 15*th*, 18

DEAR LORD WHITWORTH,

As I owe my trip to Paris in great measure to the kindne
and readiness with which you dispensed with my services
Ireland—it is but just that I should give you some account
my proceedings—Croker, Fitzgerald and myself left Town
Saturday Morning last [8th] arrived at Dover that night. I wa
a little disappointed to hear that the Tricolor Flag was flyin
at Calais—However we were determined, perhaps rathe
rashly—to make an attempt to land, and sailed the ne
morning in an armed schooner—putting the guns below an
hoisting a flag of truce when we got into Calais roads. Th
Governor however was inexorable—and positively refused
permission to land. We heard that the white flag was flyin
at Dunkirk and at Boulogne and the wind favoured for th
latter—we made for it. As we passed Vimereux and Amble
teuse we saw the white flag flying there and indeed at ever
intervening village between Calais and Boulogne. It was la
in the evening when we arrived off Boulogne—we could di
cern that there was a flag hoisted, and on standing in close int
the harbour we found it was the Tricolor.

Fitzgerald and I were so sick and heartily tired of our
vage, that we resisted most strenuously Croker's proposition
make for Dieppe—we wrote a very civil note to the Com-
ndant—hoisted our flag of Truce and despatched a
ssenger. He was detained about three hours—he said that
r arrival in the roads had caused great alarm in the garrison
hat he had been placed under arrest on his landing—had
en taken to the Commandant who was holding a sort of
uncil of war—that the flag of truce was mistaken for the
ite flag—particularly as the Schooner was armed—and unfor-
ately for us three or four English Brigs were in the offing.
However he brought with him a civil answer from the
mmandant informing us that "une mesure de sureté
litaire l'occupoit à le moment," but when he was at leisure
would send a boat for us.

We were half afraid to trust ourselves to him, particularly
he told our envoy that he could not recognize a flag of truce
an armed vessel, but the apprehension of a sail to Dieppe
th a contrary wind overcame the apprehension of a day or
o's confinement at Boulogne. The boat arrived—and we
ided at Boulogne about 3 o'clcok on Monday morning. The
mmandant was civil to us but did not conceal from us that
was a furious Bonapartist. He said he had no soldiers—if
had 30 that white flag in the next village should not be
isted—or there should be a massacre if it was. We pro-
ded on our journey about 7 o'clock on the morning of
onday—nothing could exceed the apparent devotion of all
e inhabitants of the country through which we passed to the
use of Louis—the white flag was hanging from every win-
w. Vive le Roi was in every mouth. We met with no inter-
ption until we arrived at Montreuil—where there was a
ong garrison—the Commandant like the officers—deter-
ned Bonapartists. We had nothing but Castlereagh's pass-
rt except La Chatre's which was worse than nothing, but
e Commandant allowed us after some parley to proceed.
e presence of the military was hardly sufficient to keep
wn the popular feeling in favour of the King—among the
abitants it was universal here as every where else, there
s not a single exception. At Abbeville we were again stopped.
ere there was a very strong garrison—2000 men. Party spirit
s running very high. The inhabitants were armed—the
litary seemed disposed to resist the order which they

expected to receive on the day of our arrival, to lay down th
arms and leave the town.

Every precaution was taken as if the town was besieg
There were soldiers at every drawbridge. The Command
however allowed us to proceed—and we arrived safely at P
on the evening of Tuesday.

Sunday, 16*th*.

Paris is surrounded by the troops of the allies and noth
can be more interesting than the present situation of it. T
streets are crowded with officers and soldiers of all natio
Cossacks—Russians—Prussians, Austrians, Hungarians, e
The English are great favourites. The Prussians held in
greatest detestation. If they had entered Paris alone—or if t
Crowned Heads had delayed their entry—they, the Prussi
would probably have pillaged Paris. They have taken so
pictures from the Louvre—a very few, however, and none
which they had not some claim. They have demanded t
payment of one hundred millions of francs from the city a
at this moment—there are Prussian guards in the houses
Perigaux and some of the other principal bankers who
held as a sort of hostage—for the payment of the contributi

We drove to-day to the Depot d'Artillerie, and were t
by the sentry—one of the national guards, that we were w
come to see the salon—but that the Prussians had remov
everything which it contained—the sword of Joan of Arc
the knife of Ravaillac—Tureene's sword. I am sorry for this
not on account of the mortification which it will inflict
French vanity—but because I fear the return of the King v
be less popular—than it would have been if he could ha
preserved entire at least those national monuments and rel
which are exclusively French.

We paid a visit to Denon the other day. He had some Pru
sians quartered upon him, and was very loud in his exclam
tions against *ce* [sic] *bête féroce* as he called Blucher. E
expressed his sentiments very freely on political subjects
said the King was not destined to govern France in times li
these—and predicted a short duration to his dynasty. E
spoke in terms of great and apparently sincere affecti
towards Bonaparte—he was the last person who saw h
before he quitted Paris. Denon observed that he had co
mitted a great error after the battle of Waterloo in quitting t
army—that he had by that step lost its confidence—that

ght either to have remained with it—or to have returned to
immediately. If he had summoned the two chambers, in-
med them without reserve of his disasters and concluded
stating that his travelling carriage was at the door and that
was going to resume the command of the army, that even
l he need not have despaired of ultimate success.

At the Tuileries after mass there was a great collection of
arshals—Peers of France—and other rogues of the higher
ler. We saw Marmont—Macdonald—Masséna—St. Cyr—
upont, etc., and almost all the General officers of the French
ny who are in Paris—and did not take a decided part
ainst the King. The garden of the Tuileries was absolutely
l of people, and nothing can exceed or describe the en-
usiasm of the women and children in favour of the King.
shouts—and applause and Vive le Roi—and white handker-
iefs could contribute to his strength—his throne would be
ablished on solid foundations, but I do not see that men—
hting men—partake so much of the general joy—I confess
think the King has been ill advised in making Fouché his
ief confidant and minister. It seems to me that it must pre-
ade him from punishing treason in others—if he rewards so
torious a traitor as Fouché so highly. Fouché betrayed the
ng—then he betrayed Bonaparte—then he betrayed
ovisional Government of which he was the head and now
is minister. In fact he betrayed the Provisional Government
liberately—and on condition that he should be the King's
viser. The virulence of French traitors—owing to the im-
nity of Treason—is beyond conception. Grouchy has
itten a letter to the Emperor of Russia requesting him to
tercede in his favour with the King—and to procure for him
rmission to retain his rank as Marshal in the French army
, if that cannot be granted, that the Emperor will allow him
enter the Russian army retaining his present rank. The
mperor's answer was not amiss. He had nothing to say to his
st Proposition—and with respect to his second—it was an
dispensable qualification in a Russian officer that he should
e a man of honour.

Pray remember me very kindly to the Duchess of Dorset
d believe me ever

Dear Lord Whitworth,

is Excellency   Yours most truly

The Lord Lieutenant.   ROBERT PEEL.

PARIS, *Monday, July 1*

Arbuthnot saw Mr. Lane about an hour since I had account from him—$\frac{1}{2}$ past 3.

Mr. Lane of No. 5 Essex Court in the Temple states him to have arrived to-day from France; and he gives the follow account:

That on the 20th he left Paris, and notwithstanding th were firing of guns and other marks of rejoicing, there wa general feeling in the town that all was not going well; that Boulogne Mr. Lane saw the *Moniteur* of the 22nd which gi a long account of what is called the battle of Marenna stating that the British were 90,000 men and the French so many, that until four in the Evening the French had co pletely won the battle, but that about that hour the Engl Cavalry had attacked the Cuirrassiers and routed them, t the young guards coming to their assistance got entangled their confusion, and the old guard was likewise "*entrainé* At this moment some *Malveillant* in the army cried "Sau qui peut" and a general flight commenced; the whole l wing of the army *dispersed*: He lost all his cannon caissons, e Buonaparte had ordered the wreck of his army to be collect near Phillipville, and he had issued directions calling on Northern provinces to rise in mass. This, says the *Monite* ended a battle so glorious yet so fatal to the French arr Buonaparte has arrived in Paris on the morning of the 21 The Council of Ministers and the two chambers had be placed in a state of permanency and it was declared hi treason to vote an adjournment.

Extract of a letter from the DUKE *of* WELLINGTON
to SIR CHARLES FLINT.

dated BRUSSELS.

19 *June* 18

What do you think of the total defeat of Bonaparte by t British Army?

Never was there in the annals of the World so desperate so hard fought an action, or such a defeat. It was really t battle of the Giants.

My heart is broken by the terrible loss I have sustained my old friends and companions and my poor Soldiers; and shall not be satisfied with this Battle however glorious, if does not of itself put an end to Bonaparte.

have been asked for so many Copies of this (all of which I
ve refused) that I am glad to return it.]

19 *June* 1815.

On the 16th to the very great astonishment of everyone the
ench attacked us or rather the Prussians, Lord Wellington
me up with a very few Troops including the 7 Divisions and
cceeded in stopping them, the next day was passed in partial
ivalry actions and yesterday was fought the severest battle
at I believe ever has been known, the disproportion was
mense so much so that altho' we constantly repulsed them
t had not the Prussians come up at 7 (altho' in fact they
ight have been up long before) we perhaps might ultimately
ve been annihilated. Trotter and I was on the field at the
ginning and I count it as the best day of my life—I was
ere also to-day—the French have abandoned everything—
point of Artillery it is a second Vittoria.

Our loss is so great that our Army will not I fear be in a
ite to act efficiently—but as we have done the material thing,
e Allies may do the rest—the French Cavalry which was
ry fine suffered beyond expression—For a mile the road is
tually strewed with Cuirasses—when I say this, I do not
aggerate. The Prussians are pursuing as fast as they can and
ith a large body of Troops. There will not be a stop by possi-
lity till we get over the Frontier, after that time I dare not
ophesy, but I do not think they will like to attack us again.
The Action was fought in front of *Waterloo* where two
oads separate—the one going to Nivelle, the other to
enappe—the position which was a very beautiful one was
front of the junction of the two roads. [*unsigned.*]

The great action of yesterday was the severest contest either
renchmen or Englishmen ever witnessed—it was the most
ostinate struggle of two brave and rival Nations each firm in
s cause—The gallantry of the French could only be ex-
eded by the resolution and intrepidity of John Bull. It raged
om 11 till 9 and was once nearly lost. The Duke seconded
y his Troops repaired every momentary disaster.

Buonaparte placed himself at the head of his guards and led
em on. The 1st Guards defeated them and put them to the
ut and then the dismay became general—The Guards and
enerally the Infantry were the mainstay of the Action. Our

Brigade had the defence of a Post which if lost, lost all. O
Light Company under Colonel Macdonnell were there, t
Coldstreams then went down and we held it to the last, th
the Houses were in Flames. The loss has been immense
The French are totally defeated.

There never was a more severe Battle than that of the 18
I enclose a little Sketch of it. The dotted Line from Braine
Leud to above La Haye is the brow of the Hills occupied
the Duke of Wellington. The Troops had bivouaced just
the rear. The other dotted line near La Belle Alliance mar
the brow of the Hills from where the French attack was mad
There are two small Hedges in the Rear of this one. T
Attack on Hougomont was very severe from a little befo
12 to half past one. Bonaparte then moved a strong For
(continuing however his first Attack for several hours)
attack the left of the Centre where Picton and Ponsonby we
killed. He drove our people from the Hedges a short distan
but they soon returned and drove him considerably beyo
those Hedges. In the Evening he collected a very great for
near La Haye Sainte and attacked the Right of the Cent
This was done repeatedly by Infantry and Cavalry but thou
they frequently got through the Line they could never dri
them from their position. The British Artillery was a little
front. The Duke several times left the Guns taking away t
Horses and Ammunition, but his Fire was too heavy for t
Enemy to bring up Horses to take them off and he as oft
regained them. At about 7 o'clock the French were heart
sick of it and retired rapidly. The Duke immediately chang
his Defensive operations to that of Attack and at the san
time Bulow brought up about 30,000 fresh Troops on t
right flank of the Enemy near the Village of La Haye. Bluch
was also near at hand.

The Rout at this time was complete. The Pursuit was rap
and I really believe that the following morning the Fren
Army had not 50 Guns out of 300 and no Baggage of any so

The latter part of this Account I take from others and fro
seeing the Field of Battle two days afterwards. The first ar
second attacks I was present at.

The Returns are arrived of Killed and Wounded. T
British and Hanoverians lost on the 16th, 17th and 18th 8
Officers and 13,000 Men. The French lost much more. T
Method in which the Duke received the united Charges

valry and attacks of Infantry is not common. He formed
o Regiments in Squares and united them by a Regt. in Line
ur deep making a Sort of Curtain between two Bastions.
nsigned.]

§ iii

After Lord Whitworth's term of office had come to an end
and the duchess returned to live at Knole, and to make such
mprovements as there were agreeable to the taste of the early
neteenth century. Such were the Gothic windows of the
rangery, which replaced the Tudor ones and were inscribed
th the date 1823, and further changes were projected, such
a design which was to sweep away the symmetry of the
wns on the garden front and bring a curving path up to the
use. This scheme, however, was never carried out. The
wling-green still rises, square and formal, backed by the
o great tulip trees and the more distant woods of the park.
he long perspective of the herbaceous borders was left un-
sturbed. The apple-trees in the little square orchards, that
ar their blossom and their fruit from year to year with such
untrified simplicity in the heart of all that magnificence,
ere not uprooted. Consequently the garden, save for one
all section where the paths curve in meaningless scollops
nong the rhododendrons, remains to-day very much as Anne
lifford knew it. It has, of course, matured. The white rose
hich was planted under James I's room has climbed until it
w reaches beyond his windows on the first floor; the great
ne has drooped its branches until they have layered them-
lves in the ground of their own accord and grown up again
th fresh roots into three complete circles all sprung from the
rent tree, a cloister of limes, which in summer murmurs like
e enormous bee-hive; the magnolia outside the Poets' Par-
ur has grown nearly to the roof, and bears its mass of flame-
aped blossoms like a giant candelabrum; the beech hedge is
venty feet high; four centuries have winnowed the faultless
rf. In spring the wistaria drips its fountains over the top of
e wall into the park. The soil is rich and deep and old. The
rden has been a garden for four hundred years.

And here, save for a few very brief notes to bring the histo
of the house down to the present day, these sketches mu
cease. The duchess Arabella Diana dying in 1825, her esta
devolved upon her two daughters, Mary and Elizabet
Elizabeth, my great-grandmother, who married John We
Lord de la Warr, and who died in 1870, left Buckhurst to h
elder sons and Knole to her younger sons, one of whom w
my grandfather. He was, as I remember him, a queer a
silent old man. He knew nothing whatever about the works
art in the house; he spent hours gazing at the flowers, follow
about the garden by two grave demoiselle cranes; he turn
his back on all visitors, but sized them up after they had go
in one shrewd and sarcastic phrase; he bore a really remarkal
resemblance to the portraits of the old Lord Treasurer, a
he seemed to me, with his taciturnity and the never-mention
background of his own not unromantic past, to stand co
formably at the end of the long line of his ancestors. He and
who so often shared the house alone between us, were cor
panions in a shy and undemonstrative way. Although he h
nothing to say to his unfortunate guests, he could understa
a child. He told me that there were underground caves in tl
Wilderness, and I believed him to the extent of digging pi
among the laurels in the hope of chancing upon the entranc
he made over a tall tree to me for my own, and I mounted
wooden cannon among its branches to keep away intrude
When I was away, which was seldom, he would write m
harlequin letters in different coloured chalks. When I was
home he would put after dinner a plate of fruit for my brea
fast into a drawer of his writing-table labelled with my nam
and this he never once failed to do, even though there mig
have been thirty people to dinner in the Great Hall, wl
watched, no doubt with great surprise, the old man who h
been so rude to his neighbours at dinner going unconcerned
round with a plate, picking out the reddest cherries, the blue
grapes, and the ripest peach.

When we were at Knole alone together, I used to go dow
to his sitting-room in the evening to play draughts with him
and never knew whether I played to please him, or he playe

please me—and sometimes, very rarely, he told me stories
when he was a small boy, and played with the rocking-horse,
of the journeys by coach with his father and mother from
ckhurst to Knole or from Knole to London; of their taking
silver with them under the seat; of their having outriders
h pistols; and of his father and mother never addressing
h other, in their children's presence, as anything but "my
d" and "my Lady." I clasped my knees and stared at him
en he told me these stories of an age which already seemed
emote, and his pale blue eyes gazed away into the past, and
denly his shyness would return to him and the clock in the
ner would begin to wheeze in preparation to striking the
ir, and he would say that it was time for me to go to bed.
: although our understanding of one another was, I am
e, so excellent, our rare conversations remained always on
ilar fantastic subjects, nor ever approached the intimate or
personal.

hen he fell ill and died when he was over eighty, and
ame a name like the others, and his portrait took its place
ong the rest, with a label recording the dates of his birth
death.

Appendix 1

A NOTE ON THIEVES' CANT

ɪE VOCABULARY given on page 136 contributes no word which
ɑy not be found in any cant dictionary, and therefore may
pear undeserving of inclusion. But I put it in because I
ɪnk few people, apart from students of philology, realize the
ɪstence of that large section of our language in use among
ɪ vagabond classes. Cant and slang, to most people's minds,
ɪ synonymous, but this is an error of belief: slang creeps
ɪm many sources into the river of language, and so mingles
ɪth it that in course of time many use it without knowing
ɑt they do so; cant, on the other hand, remains definite and
ɪscure of origin. Slang is loose, expressive, and metaphorical;
ɪnt is tight and correct; it has even a literature of its own,
ɪoad and racy, incomprehensible to the ordinary reader
ɪthout the help of a glossary. Its words, for the most part,
ɪar no resemblance to English words; unlike slang, they are
ɪt words adapted, for the sake of vividness, to a use for which
ɪey were not originally intended, but are applied strictly to
ɪeir peculiar meaning.

Although the origin of cant as a separate jargon or language
ɪ obscure—it does not appear in England till the second
ɪlf of the sixteenth century—the origin of certain of its
ɪrds may be traced. Of those included in the vocabulary,
ɪr example, *ken*, for house, comes from *khan* (gipsy and
ɪriental); *fogus*, for tobacco, comes from *fogo*, an old word for
ɪnch; *maund*, or *maunder*, to beg, does not derive, as might
ɪ thought, from *maung*, to beg, a gipsy word taken from the
ɪndu, but from the Anglo-Saxon *mand*, a basket; *bouse*, to
ɪnk (which, of course, has given us booze, with the same
ɪeaning, and which in the fourteenth century was perfectly
ɪod English), comes from the Dutch *buyzen*, to tipple.
ɪram*, naked, is found as *abrannoi*, with the same meaning, in

Hungarian gipsy; *cassan*, cheese, is *cas* in English gip
dimber survives for "pretty" in Worcestershire. *Cheat* appe
frequently in cant as a common affix.

As for *autem mort*, I find it in an early authority thus define
"These *autem morts* be married women, as there be but a fe
For *autem* in their language is a church, so she is a wife ma
ried at the church, and they be as chaste as a cow I have, th
goeth to bull every moon, with what bull she careth not."

ᴀᴠᴇ to record with sorrow that Knole was given over to the
tional Trust in 1947. It was the only thing to do, and as a
ential inheritor of Knole I had to sign documents giving
ole away. It nearly broke my heart, putting my signature
what I couldn't help regarding as a betrayal of all the
dition of my ancestors and the house I loved.

deeply respect and admire the National Trust and all that it
es for the salvation of properties. I don't know where we
uld be without it. I should, however, like to reprint an article
rote in the *Spectator* which will perhaps reflect the feelings
many other people who have had to hand over their home
ause they were no longer able to afford to keep it up.

n times when the esteem of beauty and the humanities
es like an unhonoured nymph from the eyes of men; times
en expediency, convenience, and economy demand and
d our entire and sole consideration; times when pressure
npels us to forget that "Beauty being the best of all we
w. Sums up unsearchable and secret aims"; times when
uty and all that stands for culture make no more impact
men's ears than the unreality of a dead language—in such
es it comes as a plumb luxury to indulge even for a moment
the contemplation of something so very different, some-
ng so unnecessary, so inordinate, prodigal, extravagant,
traditional, as the great houses of the past. Of the past
y are indeed, not only in century but in spirit; anachronisms
h in time and in tenure. Yet in their growth they were
anic, and in their creation they involved the completion of
ny a human life, the life of the craftsman who laboured,
stone-mason, the carver, the carpenter, the builder of
mneys, and the life also of those who ordered and enjoyed,
obscure "Richards, Johns, Annes, Elizabeths, not one of
om has left a token of himself behind him, yet all, working
ether with their spades and their needles, their love-
king and their child-bearing, have left this."

Thus wrote Virginia Woolf of those who had made Kn
and it seems to me, whose home it was and whom am
greatly moved by the merest thought of it to write or think
it with sufficient objectivity, that she has put her fingers
the still living truth of this massive anachronism. They h
left this. They, a living stream of men and women w
laboured, suffered, loved, were ordinary, and cared for bea
and the gracious way. What, then, is this house which rose
gradually stone by stone quarried from its native county, a
what is its significance either in the past or in the future?
an agglomeration of stones a soul-less thing? Does it breat
does it live, does it hold a spirit of its own even as every s
has her own temper? Bacon made the subtle and profou
remark that there was "no excellent beauty that hath
some strangeness in the proportion," but this is not true
Knole, which in every sobriety of proportion proclaims t
straightforwardness of design and colour may also comp
into a perfection, homogenous though diversified, with
oddity, as continuous as history itself. History indeed is i
plicit here, for behind the roughest earliest portion wh
served as a tithe-barn in the days of Magna Carta, has gro
up the vast structure which after soaring to its peak of po
as a palace of the Archbishop of Canterbury and a palace
the Crown, then became for many generations the home of
English family and now in the days of democracy is about
pass into the possession of the nation for the enjoyment of
people. There it lies, grey, silent, and inscrutable. Few of
many chimney-stacks now send up their thread of smoke,
its population is diminished and this blue symbolic breath
its life has faded down with the death of the different mode
existence that went to its making. Great state was observ
here once, when well over a hundred servants sat down da
to eat at long tables in the Great Hall; the very list of th
employments suggests the sound and activity which stir
within the walls of this self-contained encampment, t
private burg: the armourer, the falconer, the slaughterm
the brewer, the baker, the barber, the huntsman, the yeom
of the granary, the farrier, the grooms of the great horse, a
the stranger's horse, the men to carry wood, Solomon
bird-catcher, and many others besides, all coming in from th
bothies and outhouses to share in the communal meal w
their master, his lady, their children, their guests, and

b of indoor servants whose avocations ranged from His
rdship's Favourite through innumerable pages, attendants,
ooms and yeomen of various chambers, scriveners, pantry-
n, maids, clerks of the kitchen and the buttery, down to
e humble Grace Robinson and John Morockoe, both
ackamoors. Some of their names, I think, would have
eased Thomas Hardy: Penelope Tutty, Faith Husband, and
idow Ben among the women; and among the men Paschal
ard, Moses Shonk, Diggory Dyer and Marfidy Snipt.
uests came and went, standing out as more illustrious above
is contributory rabble: John Donne, who preached sermons
Archbishop Cranmer's chapel; John Dryden, who profited
om the munificence of the master of Knole, himself a poet;
atthew Prior who owed his education to that same master;
eeting together and talking and drinking in a room described
· Horace Walpole as "a chamber of parts and players, which
proper enough in that house." Guests came and went; and
w they have for ever gone. They will come no more, neither
ey nor their present counterparts, and that which was a
ing thing with its granaries, its chapel, its larders and still-
oms, its ruffle and talk, the hooves ringing on the stable-
rd, the rhymesters cadging in the Poets' Parlour, the long
rden-paths made for twilight pacing and deliberation, will
ange over into some new transformation of itself, but what
is transmigration of soul will bring about we cannot tell.
remains to be seen. As birth is a process of pain, so must
birth be a process of pain also; one is prepared to accept the
in, in the hope that the travail will suscitate some Phoenix
future value. Poets will no longer have to depend for their
ucation and opportunity on the whim of a patron, nor will
e privilege of beauty be reserved for the few who can afford
indulge it. But what of those to whom these things belonged
· birthright, and who belonged to the service of these things
tradition? Shall they weep over the passing, or shall they
ltivate the philosophy that the old world must with cheer-
lness relinquish its heritage into the hands of the new? Do
ey not deserve a word, if only a word of valediction? It is a
all thing, perhaps; only a single feather observed falling
om the too gorgeous plumage of the discarded past; but to
em it is the sacrifice, the symbol, of something perhaps too
ofoundly dear. For their comfort, let us suggest that some
· the grace of another age may seep into the consciousness of

the million wandering freely among these ancient cou
and that the new young Richards, Johns, Annes, and Eli
beths (who also are a part of continuous history) may f
enrichment in the gift of something so old, so courteous, a
so lovely.

INDEX

*Printed in Great Britain by Offset Litho
by Cox & Wyman Ltd, London, Fakenham and Reading*